Kenosis and Its Power

Kenosis and Its Power

The Kyoto School, Contemporary Philosophy, Political Theology

EDITED BY
NORIHITO NAKAMURA

☙PICKWICK *Publications* • Eugene, Oregon

KENOSIS AND ITS POWER
The Kyoto School, Contemporary Philosophy, Political Theology

Copyright © 2025 Norihito Nakamura. All rights reserved. Except for brief quotations in critical publications or reviews, no part of this book may be reproduced in any manner without prior written permission from the publisher. Write: Permissions, Wipf and Stock Publishers, 199 W. 8th Ave., Suite 3, Eugene, OR 97401.

Pickwick Publications
An Imprint of Wipf and Stock Publishers
199 W. 8th Ave., Suite 3
Eugene, OR 97401

www.wipfandstock.com

PAPERBACK ISBN: 979-8-3852-2714-3
HARDCOVER ISBN: 979-8-3852-2715-0
EBOOK ISBN: 979-8-3852-2716-7

Cataloguing-in-Publication data:

Names: Nakamura, Norihito, editor.

Title: Kenosis and its power : the Kyoto school, contemporary philosophy, political theology / edited by Norihito Nakamura.

Description: Eugene, OR : Pickwick Publications, 2025 | Includes bibliographical references.

Identifiers: ISBN 979-8-3852-2714-3 (paperback) | ISBN 979-8-3852-2715-0 (hardcover) | ISBN 979-8-3852-2716-7 (ebook)

Subjects: LCSH: Kyoto school. | Incarnation. | Philosophical theology. | Philosophy, Japanese—20th century.

Classification: BR128.B8 .K40 2025 (paperback) | BR128.B8 (ebook)

10/17/25

Emphasis added to Scripture quotations.

Scripture quotations marked KJV are from the King James or Authorized Version.

Scripture quotations marked NRSV are from the New Revised Standard Version, copyright © 1989, Division of Christian Education of the National Council of the Churches of Christ in the United States of America. Used by permission. All rights reserved.

Scripture quotations marked ESV are from the ESV® Bible (The Holy Bible, English Standard Version®), copyright © 2001 by Crossway, a publishing ministry of Good News Publishers. ESV Text Edition: 2016. Used by permission. All rights reserved.

Scripture quotations marked NRSVue are from the New Revised Standard Version, Updated Edition, copyright © 2021 National Council of Churches of Christ in the United States of America. Used by permission. All rights reserved worldwide.

Contents

Abbreviations vii

Introduction ix

PART I. KENOSIS IN POLITICAL THEOLOGY AND CONTINENTAL PHILOSOPHY

1   Kenosis as a Life-Form in Polycrisis: Universalization by Naturalization or Metaphorical Thinking?   3
Norihito Nakamura

2   Kenosis: Towards a Political Theology of Love   18
Saitya Brata Das

3   *Mystici Corpori*: From the Kenotic Christ to the Kenotic Church—Fragments of a Grand Narrative   33
Tobias Bartneck

4   Kenosis in Contemporary Continental Philosophy: From Deconstruction to Phenomenology   49
Nikolaas Cassidy-Deketelaere

PART II. KENOSIS IN THE KYOTO SCHOOL AND THE NON-WESTERN TRADITION

5   A Hidden Japanese Source of Kenosis in Contemporary Christian Theology? Kyoto School, Kazo Kitamori, and Jürgen Moltmann   73
Yusuke Okada

CONTENTS

6   The Kenosis of the Rational: Tanabe Hajime's Philosophical Failure and the Violent Implications of Human Rationality   91
Satoshi Urai

7   Kenosis: A Dialogue Between Nicholas of Cusa and Nishitani Keiji   111
Myriam-Sonja Hantke

8   Kenosis, Dynamic *Śūnyatā*, and Weak Thought: Abe Masao and Gianni Vattimo   130
Thorsten Botz-Bornstein

Abbreviations

HAA	Heidelberger Akademie Ausgabe
HeyJ	*Heythrop Journal*
IR	自覚に於ける直観と反省 [Intuition and reflection in self-consciousness]. By Kitarō Nishida. Tokyo: Iwanami, 1917
NA[28]	*Novum Testamentum Graece,* Nestle-Aland, 28th ed.
RHPR	*Revue d'histoire et de philosophie religieuses*
THZ	Tanabe, Hajime. 『田辺元全集』[Complete works of Tanabe Hajime]. 15 vols. Tokyo: Chikuma Shobō, 1963–64.
NKZ	Nishida, Kitarō. 『西田幾多郎全集』 [Complete works of Nishida Kitarō]. 15 vols. Tokyo: Iwanami Shoten, 1963–64.

Introduction

WHAT IS KENOSIS? To put it generally and concisely, *kenosis* is a Christian theological concept that refers to the "self-emptying" of Jesus. Jesus, while being fully divine, voluntarily emptied himself and renounced certain divine privileges and powers. This idea is primarily drawn from Phil 2:5–8, where Paul describes Christ humbling himself by taking on human form and accepting death on the cross.

This concept has sparked extensive theological discussions over its long history, but its meaning underwent a transformation in the twentieth century. In an era of modernity as nihilism, where secularization and the death of God are taken for granted, kenosis prompts us to consider a new form of religion. We could formulate this transformation as a *kenosis of kenosis*. What does this mean? It means that kenosis could never have attained its true *power* in a time when Christianity was more dominant and privileged. One could say that in the age of globalization, when Christianity or monotheistic religion in general is relativized by other religions, kenosis, the core of Christianity, renounced its own privileged status and opened a path for dialogue with a variety of other religions and cultures. This volume of essays aims to open up the philosophical and historical significance of this kenosis of kenosis.

This volume of essays is divided into two parts: the first part consists of analyses of kenosis from the perspectives of political theology and contemporary philosophy. The second part focuses on the Japanese philosophers of the Kyoto School and consists of studies of the interreligious potential of kenosis.

Part 1, "Kenosis in Political Theology and Continental Philosophy," consists of four articles. In the first article, Nakamura examines the implications of an interreligious and intercultural reinterpretation of kenosis in our age of *polycrisis*. This essay provides a critical reading of the work of Sallie McFague, a contemporary ecological theologian. The second article, by Das, adventurously speculates, through a deep reading of Paul's words, that the enigma of love suggested by kenosis could dissolve the nomos of the secular order. The third article by Bartneck addresses the relationship between the self-emptying of Christ and the Roman Catholic Church as his "mystical body" through an interpretation of Nishitani, Gauchet, and others. The fourth article, by Cassidy-Deketelaere, surveys two major currents in the contemporary philosophy of religion—postsecularism and the theological turn in phenomenology—and explores the project of the "phenomenology of kenosis" in the philosophy of Jean-Luc Nancy, which goes beyond these currents.

Part 2, "Kenosis in the Kyoto School and the Non-Western Tradition," also consists of four articles. In the fifth article, Okada addresses the notion of the kenotic God in the Kyoto School. Here, Okada shows that Kitaro Nishida, the founder of the Kyoto School, referred to "kenosis" in his final writings, and that his disciple Kitamori, a Christian theologian in postwar Japan, developed it further. Kitamori's "Theology of the Pain of God" was embraced by Moltmann, who enthusiastically advanced the theology of kenosis in the late twentieth century. The sixth article, by Urai, focuses on the philosophy of Hajime Tanabe, Nishida's disciple and rival. Here Urai shows that Tanabe's criticism of modern rationality suggests the kenotic nature of his philosophy. Hantke, in the seventh essay, compares the philosophy of Nicholas of Cusa, the origin of kenotic theology, with that of Keiji Nishitani, the heir of the Kyoto School. The final article by Botz-Bornstein revisits the philosophy of Masao Abe, a member of the Kyoto School and a prominent Buddhist scholar well known in North America, in comparison to that of Gianni Vattimo, one of the most influential contemporary Italian philosophers. This comparison facilitates a radical encounter between *sunyata* in Zen Buddhism and kenosis in Christianity.

Before closing this introduction, I would like to describe the background of this volume. The content of this volume is primarily based on our workshop "Kenosis and Its Ethics in a Contemporary and Intercultural Perspective," held February 7–8, 2024, at the University of Tübingen, Germany. As I was organizing this workshop, I received a great deal of support from Dr.

INTRODUCTION

Niels Weidtmann, the director of the College of Fellows, and from many members of the academic staff working there. I would like to express my gratitude to them once again. Almost all of the authors in this volume participated in this workshop. Although Thorsten Botz-Bornstein is the only exception, I got to know him also at another conference in the College of Fellows. Thus, this work was born out of the *pratītya-samutpāda* (縁起, engi) of Tübingen.

While I was preparing this volume, my friend Tobias Bartneck, a contributor to this volume, passed away unexpectedly. A few days before his death, I had exchanged ideas about his article with him, so his death felt extremely sudden and upsetting to me. I had learned so much from his deep insights and wide range of knowledge, but I felt that I had not been able to properly thank him. I was initially unsure whether I should publish his unfinished article (which had already been presented at our workshop at the University of Tübingen where he graduated). However, after conversations with his family, I made the decision to publish it. I do believe that his powerful and speculative writings should be more widely read in our uncertain times.

NORIHITO NAKAMURA
Summer 2025
Kyoto and Rotterdam

PART I.

Kenosis in Political Theology and Continental Philosophy

I

Kenosis as a Life-Form in Polycrisis
Universalization by Naturalization or Metaphorical Thinking?

Norihito Nakamura

0. THE NEW LIFE-FORM OF HUMAN BEINGS IN POLYCRISIS

Today, our existence is surrounded by multiple crises: War, terrorism, economic depression, the rise of right-wing populism, pandemics, racism, gender backlash, climate change, and more. These crises are not independent of each other. For example, if environmental destruction occurs somewhere on the globe, it damages inhabitable areas and reduces food production, leading to higher prices in distant countries that depend on imported food. These factors might then lead to war, which brings refugees and immigrants to various countries. As a side effect of globalization, these risks are becoming increasingly complex and interrelated, making their consequences ever more unpredictable. The American historian Adam Tooze famously characterized this situation as a "polycrisis."

In such a context, natural scientists, economists, and politicians hold global conferences and forums every day to address these problems. While it is true that there is an urgent need to discuss immediate policies to solve them, the current crisis cannot be solved only through top-down policies from governments and bureaucrats. This polycrisis we are facing is not separate from our social existence as human beings; it should be seen as inseparable from the very life-forms and social dynamics we actually experience. As is evident when we consider the destruction of the environment, crises strike us, but at the same time, our human existence itself is a crisis for the earth.

"You must change your life." German philosopher Peter Sloterdijk gave this title to a work he published in 2009.[1] He argued for the necessity of creating a new "training system" and "life-form" for international solidarity under a paradigm that transcends the conventional dichotomy of nature and culture for people living in a global crisis today. His insight had a profound influence on Bruno Latour, who later developed his theory on Gaia and the Anthropocene. In response to their appeal, the past decade has witnessed an increase in opportunities for philosophers and humanists to engage in cooperative work with natural scientists. The recent rise of new materialism and new realism could be understood in this context.

However, while solidarity between philosophy and science has developed, I wonder if this is the case between philosophy on the one hand and religion and theology on the other. It is my impression that we do not often observe the participation of religious ethics in these new constellations of thoughts at the dawn of the twenty-first century. Nevertheless, the task of inventing some new life-form of human beings inevitably calls for a dialogue with the traditions of religion and theology. In this context, the term "kenosis" could play a significant role.

We must initiate a new game. The key to this is not to narrow the entry gate by prescribing something rigid from the beginning, but rather to start playing the game without any restrictions. It is in this free process that rules and forms will be formulated. Thus, I would like to begin a new game by treating the term "kenosis" not as a strict concept, at least initially, but as a kind of soccer ball—a way that I will later define as "metaphorical thinking."

This chapter consists of four parts. In the first part, I will introduce the basic aspects of kenosis and provide a brief history of its interpretation. In the second part, I will outline the works of Charles Taylor and Judith Butler, clarifying how their thoughts resonate with the project of Sallie McFague

---

1. Sloterdijk, *Du musst dein Leben ändern*.

(1933–2019), a contemporary American theologian who develops a theology of kenosis. This will show that our discussion on kenosis also overlaps with the work of contemporary philosophers like Taylor and Butler. In the third part, I will explore McFague's interpretation of kenosis and investigate her strategy of "naturalizing kenosis." Finally, in the fourth part, I will propose a universalization of kenosis through "metaphorical thinking," which differs from the "naturalization" implied by McFague.

To conclude briefly in advance, my position aligns with McFague in upholding the universalization of kenosis as its aim (i.e., the grounding of dialogue with natural science and various religions), but differs from her approach to the universalization of kenosis. McFague unintentionally mixed two ways of universalizing kenosis—(1) *naturalization* and (2) *metaphorical thinking*—but I believe the latter path holds greater potential for our project.

1. WHAT IS KENOSIS?

The term "kenosis" comes directly from Paul's Epistle to the Philippians in the New Testament. In its second chapter, the apostle Paul describes Jesus' act of self-sacrifice as follows:

> Let the same mind be in you that was in Christ Jesus, who, though he was in the form of God, did not regard equality with God as something to exploited, but emptied himself, taking the form of a slave, being born in human likeness. And being found in human form, he *humbled himself* and became obedient to the point of death—even death on a cross. (Phil 2:5–8 NRSV)[2]

This act of emptying himself is generally referred to as *kenosis*. Jesus, the Son of God, could have avoided becoming mortal and taking the form of a slave, but he willingly devoted his life to the salvation of others. Kenosis refers to this act of self-sacrifice and self-humiliation and, broadly, is a doctrine about its ethical meaning. Italian philosopher Diego Bubbio points out that the word "kenosis" carries three nuances that are intricately intertwined: self-limitation, self-giving, and self-emptying.[3] The semantic indeterminacy among these three concepts could dynamize the ethical implications and interpretations of kenosis.

---

2. See McFague, *Blessed Are the Consumers*, 6.
3. Bubbio, *Sacrifice in the Post-Kantian Tradition*.

PART I. KENOSIS IN POLITICAL THEOLOGY

In the context of traditional theology, the distinction between the "theology of glory" and the "theology of the cross" is significant. Broadly speaking, the former emphasizes the omnipotence of God, while the latter focuses on the finitude of God. The ethic of kenosis has long been considered the key to understanding the latter theology. This theological tradition can be traced back to Augustine, Nicholas of Cusa, Eckhart, Luther, and others. Moreover, the "theology of the cross" experienced a revival beyond the realm of dogmatics in the twentieth century. Not only theologians such as Barth, Bonhoeffer, and Hans Urs von Balthasar, but also philosophers such as Simone Weil, Levinas, and Hans Jonas began to take up and rehabilitate this term.

Although the intentions of those who have explored kenosis differ from author to author, an important fact remains: we human beings have come to realize the need for an explanation of the human and divine impotence revealed in the various catastrophes of the twentieth century. Why was no help offered to the Jews in Auschwitz? Why were the people living in Hiroshima and Nagasaki consumed by nuclear flames? What does the absence of God in such catastrophes mean? These fundamental questions emerged in the mid-twentieth century not merely as problems of doctrine and philology, but as extremely urgent, existential problems.

Jürgen Moltmann's (1926–2024) *The Crucified God* (1972) advanced the modern interpretation of kenosis one step further. From his standpoint as a theologian, Moltmann confronted the growing anxiety about nuclear war during the Cold War and the rise of environmental destruction in late capitalism. He thus reactivated the traditional concept of kenosis to engage with contemporary crises. His ecumenical readings not only fostered interreligious dialogue but also influenced political movements in South America in the form of liberation theology.

McFague, whose feminist theology I will discuss later, reinterprets this genealogy from Augustine to Moltmann to propose kenosis as a new way of life suited for an increasingly chaotic modern world. I will elaborate on this in more detail later, but for now, let me quote McFague's compact and condensed account of what kenosis means:

> In the Christian tradition, kenosis, or self-emptying, is a way of understanding God's actions in creation, the incarnation, and the cross. In creation, God limits the divine self, pulling in, so to speak, to allow space for others to exist. God, who is the one in whom we live and move and have our being, does not take all the

space but gives space and life to others. This is an inversion of the usual understanding of power as control; instead, power is given to others to live as diverse and valuable creatures.[4]

God does not reveal his glory to the world through omnipotence, but rather through self-restraint and withdrawal. McFague's emphasis lies on the paradoxical positivity brought by the passivity of withdrawal. McFague suggests that this could be an ethical guideline for living in a mass consumption society. She notes:

> In our ecological age, we now see that "being open to God" means being open to the other creatures, upon whom we depend and who depend upon us. We cannot love God unless we love God's world. Christians have always known this, because an incarnate God is a world-loving God; but now it takes on new meaning and depth as we realize the radical interrelationship and interdependence of all forms of life.[5]

2. KENOSIS IS NOT ONLY A HUMAN IDEAL BUT ALSO A NATURAL REALITY

McFague considers this way of life not merely as an ideal, but as a reality. In other words, for her, radical interrelationship and interdependence are in the essential nature of human beings. First, she criticizes the individualistic model that dates back to the eighteenth century for its tendency to overlook this interrelational human nature. She offers two models: the individualistic model and the kenotic model.[6] The former model views *autonomy* as the ideal image of human beings, while the latter model emphasizes *interdependence* as their fundamental nature.

This provides a key point of dialogue with contemporary philosophy. In this regard, two influential philosophers, Charles Taylor and Judith Butler, express views that closely align with McFague's. I offer their views here because they can help us to envision the worldview and the orientation they advocate as a critique of modern society.

In *A Secular Age*, Taylor calls the dominant image of the human being since the eighteenth-century Enlightenment the "buffered self." According

---

4. McFague, *Blessed Are the Consumers*, 7–8.
5. McFague, *Blessed Are the Consumers*, 8–9.
6. McFague, *New Climate for Christianity*, 3–10.

to him, in the modern world, human beings are or should be autonomous. It is thus assumed that it is "necessary to have confidence in our own powers of moral ordering"[7] independent of influence from the outside world. On the other hand, the "porous self," a non-mainstream image of the human being since the arrival of the modern era, is always exposed to the outside world and does not reject its influences. Under the model of the "porous self," we express ourselves in the world, with our inner and outer worlds constantly interacting with each other. By evoking this alternative image, Taylor attempts to show the expressive and spiritual dimension of the human being that has been overlooked by the monolithically historical worldview of "secularization."

Judith Butler shares the same critique of modernity, although Butler does not cite Taylor. Instead, she employs the concept of "vulnerability," which is similar to Taylor's "porous self," but which focuses on the possibility for solidarity based on vulnerability among precarious populations. In *Force of Nonviolence*, Butler begins with a critique of the social contract underlying the modern sovereign state. The subject presupposed in the social contract and the state of nature is always already imagined as a (white male) adult who is self-sufficient—as exemplified in Robinson Crusoe.[8]

However, Butler argues that this self-sufficiency is only an illusion. Needless to say, human beings are not born as adults. Instead, they depend on care from others (family, social institutions, etc.) throughout much of their lives. In this sense, interdependence is clearly an undeniable aspect of the human condition. Butler thus seeks to establish a new global concept of equality based on interdependence and vulnerability. In order to achieve this, Butler believes that it is necessary to replace the modern illusion of the state of nature with a "counter-fantasy," which she finds in psychoanalysis.[9]

These two leading philosophers of our time hold almost the quite similar critique of modernity and offer a new vision of human existence. Both of them evoke human vulnerability and affectedness, attempting to invent a model of solidarity based on human weakness. McFague's kenotic theology also aligns with their perspectives in many ways.

However, McFague radicalizes her project by extending it beyond the human dimension to encompass the natural world. For McFague, kenosis is not only an ethical ideal for human beings but the reality of the natural

---

7. Taylor, *Secular Age*, 27.
8. Butler, *Force of Nonviolence*, ch. 1.
9. Butler, *Force of Nonviolence*, 43n9.

world as such. She illustrates this idea through her discussion of the phenomenon of "nurse logs" in forests. Here I quote from her fascinating, though somewhat lengthy, description of this phenomenon:

> Nurse logs are lying-down trees—some would say dead trees—that, having lived several hundred years as standing trees, have now begun a second career as homes for other trees. The body of the nurse log provides a warm, nutrient-rich birthplace for young saplings of all sorts to grow. And it is not just seeds from the nurse tree that grow on a nurse log, but anything and everything. All are welcome! The nurse log can live another several hundred years as the giver of new life from its body. Sometimes one sees ghost nurse logs: big empty holes under the roots of trees where a nurse log used to be. The new tree stretched its roots around the nurse log and still retains this odd position after the nurse log disappears. With the hole between its roots, it is a visible sign of the tree that nurtured it. Life and death are mixed up here. What is living and what is dead? Is the nurse log dead because it is no longer standing up straight? Scarcely. Is the sapling living because it has new leaves? Yes, but barely, and only because it is living off the nurse log. It all works by symbiosis—living off one another. Nothing in an old-growth forest can go it alone; nothing could survive by itself; everything in the forest is interrelated and interdependent: all flora and fauna eat from, live from the others.[10]

Nature always already realizes interdependence. McFague suggests that many other religions also convey this message from nature to us. Religion, she argues, calls us to "move from self-centeredness to reality centeredness."[11] From this, we could say with McFague that *kenosis is realism*. Kenosis is not an act of extraordinary heroism or self-sacrifice, but the very reality in which we live. This consists in the ordinary actions that we find within our daily lives. As McFague says, "What I am suggesting is that 'kenosis,' far from being an esoteric, ancient religions practice of self-negation is, in fact, deep within the very process that created the 'individuals' we now think exist by and for themselves."[12]

---

10. McFague, *Blessed Are the Consumers*, 20–21.
11. McFague, *Blessed Are the Consumers*, 21.
12. McFague, *Blessed Are the Consumers*, 145.

PART I. KENOSIS IN POLITICAL THEOLOGY

3. DIALOGUE WITH SCIENCE: NATURALIZATION OF KENOSIS

From the above discussion, we can call McFague's attempt as a kind of "naturalization of kenosis." That is, for her, kenosis and its ethics are not unique to Christianity, but can be found in natural phenomena. Thus, she suggests such behavior must be a priori grounded in human society, which is itself a part of nature. From this vantage point, McFague offers two possibilities: (1) The first path is the possibility for a dialogue between kenotic ethics and evolutionary science. (2) The second path is the possibility for interreligious dialogue. This section addresses (1), and the next section will address (2).

The first path would be ambitious for theologians in general, but especially in North America. The well-documented conflict between Darwinism and creationism has shaped educational debates in this region, though such tensions are not confined to North America alone. For instance, in India, the National Council of Educational Research and Training, a national curriculum-setting organization, recently sought to remove the requirement that the theory of evolution be taught in elementary and junior high schools. In response to this attempt, in 2023, more than four thousand scientists signed a letter demanding that this council disclose its meeting materials.[13]

Needless to say, in order to live in a diverse society, we need to understand others with different beliefs, without abandoning our respective beliefs and worldviews. Consequently, we should also avoid inflaming conflicts between science and religion. In this regard, McFague's attempt to engage in dialogue with scientists while maintaining her position as a theologian is admirable. In guiding this dialogue, she refers to two theorists: (a) Bruno Latour and (b) Patricia Churchland. However, although McFague presents both as theoretical partners, I find her reliance on Churchland problematic.

(a) As is widely known, Latour criticized the modern dichotomies of nature and politics, science and religion, and things and people. He regards these dichotomies as a cause of our current ecological crisis. In place of the modern paradigm, he proposed a new worldview, which he called "non-modern," that treats all things as equal agents, advocating for a "political

---

13. Parvaiz, "Scientists in India."

ecology" based on this new worldview. His notion of the "Parliament of Things" is also well known.[14]

(b) McFague's other reference, Churchland, proposes a field called *neurophilosophy* or *neuroethics*, which seeks to go beyond the dualism of mind and brain. Churchland radically attempts to reconcile science and ethics in a naturalistic way. In her book *Braintrust*, she cites attachment and care between mammalian mothers and their offspring as the basis for her unification of science and ethics. "In brief, the idea is that attachment, underwritten by the painfulness of separation and the pleasure of company, and managed by intricate neural circuitry and neurochemicals, is the neural platform for morality."[15] From this passage, we could immediately wonder if she naively falls into a "naturalistic fallacy," reducing all moral descriptions of "what we should do" to natural descriptions of "what we are." In fact, she embraces reductionism: "In the most basic sense, . . . caring is a ground-floor function of nervous systems."[16]

From this, we should ask whether we can reconcile (a) Latour's position with (b) Churchland's. It is true that both seem to agree on the same goal of overcoming the dualism of nature and culture, or science and nonscience. However, in many ways they are clearly different. I will not go into the details of their differences, but the most important difference is that Latour would not accept reductionism through science. On the contrary, early in his career, he investigated experiments in the natural sciences from an anthropological perspective, focusing on the discursive dimension behind seemingly purely scientific theory-building. Thus, to be precise, Latour focused on the *hybridity* of nature and culture rather than their primordial *unity*. In other words, nature and culture, science and religion, and objects and people are inherently inextricably intertwined networks themselves. Unfortunately, McFague does not seem to place much of an emphasis on the differences between these two theorists.

Now, we must reconsider the strategy of naturalizing kenosis in order to universalize it. Obviously, McFague and Churchland differ in their procedures. The former focused on the kenosis performed in natural forests, while the latter focused on the care relationships and interdependence of mammals. However, they both share the same goal of naturalizing their own ethics. Then, should we, with McFague, justify kenosis as naturalistic?

14. Latour, *We Have Never Been Modern*.
15. Churchland, *Braintrust*, 16; quoted in McFague, *Blessed Are the Consumers*, 124.
16. McFague, *Blessed Are the Consumers*, 124.

PART I. KENOSIS IN POLITICAL THEOLOGY

4. INTERRELIGIOUS DIALOGUE THROUGH METAPHORICAL THINKING

To offer my own conclusion at the outset of this section, I believe it is possible to universalize kenosis without taking the naturalistic path. Perhaps what is at issue here is the difference between *viewing kenosis as a natural phenomenon and as a metaphor* in the broad sense. My position is the second path. That is, we do kenosis "as" the forest does kenosis. Or, as Jesus does kenosis, so the forest does kenosis. This "as" or "like" is essential here. We can do kenosis without knowing it as a concept or principle. We can also do kenosis without knowing and understanding Christian doctrine, the actions of Jesus, or the Bible because we do so in a metaphorical sense.

To put it more boldly, while *fundamental (originary) thinking* is oriented toward identity and sameness (naturalism falls into this category), *metaphorical thinking* is oriented toward similarity and correspondence. The latter could be the "art of translation" that allows two things to interact without being exactly the same. In other words, the metaphor of kenosis makes it possible to link—through analogy—various events and ideas that have not been compared before. This will lead to an alternative understanding of universality, one that is different from the universal grounding of nature or the universe. When McFague referred to "nurse logs" for universalizing kenosis, she was probably unaware of the difference between fundamental and metaphorical thinking. However, I find in her though a latent potential for the possibility of metaphorical thinking.[17]

Building on this, I would like to bring up, finally, the fact that McFague regarded kenosis as a key concept for interreligious dialogue. As an entry point to this theme, I turn to McFague's distinction between "the spirituality of addition" and "the spirituality of subtraction."[18] The spirituality of addition is "the capitalist version, leaving the ego in the center and adding to it in consumer fashion," while the spirituality of subtraction means "letting go; how to let go of our security, our good reputation, our identity and

---

17. The shift in philosophical interest from concept to metaphor is found in Blumenberg and others, but I cannot go into it here.

18. This is a distinction made by Franciscan Richard Rohr (McFague, *Blessed Are the Consumers*, 152).

our self-image."[19] She reformulates this distinction as the tension between property as a power and letting go as a power.[20]

McFague points out that this "spirituality of subtraction" can be found in various religions. She cites the following examples:

> (Buddhism) "Whoever in this world overcomes his selfish cravings, his sorrow fall [sic] away from him, like drops of water from a lotus flower." (Dhammapada 336)
> (Christianity) "No one can be slave of two masters.... You cannot be the slave both of God and money." (Matt 6:24)
> (Confucianism) "Excess and deficiency are equally at fault." (Confucius 11.15)
> (Daoism) "He who knows he has enough is rich." (Dao De Jing)
> (Hinduism) "That person who lives completely free from desires, without longing ... attains peace." (Bhagavad Gita 2.71).
> (Islam) "Eat and drink, but waste not by excess: He loves not the excessive." (Qur'an 7:31)
> (Judaism) "Give me neither poverty nor riches." (Prov 30:8)[21]

Needless to say, other religions do not use the word "kenosis." However, McFague believes they all teach an ethical way of life through "subtracting," and in that respect each of them echoes the other. The Daoist subtracts from his wealth as the Christian subtracts from his wealth; the Muslim subtracts from his wealth as the Daoist does, and so on. Alternatively, we could say that as Jesus did kenosis, so does the Daoist subtract his wealth. Or, as Jesus did kenosis, so too did Lao Tzu Wu-Wei, and so on.

McFague notes also that many religions do indeed develop an ethic of "self-restraint," but they do not logically persuade or force others to follow that ethic. Instead, they present a "path to self-restraint." In other words, religion is not necessarily a philosophical principle, but the call "you must change your life" that arises from illustrations of the lives of great teachers and saints. Although McFague does not frame it in this way, we could say that religion does not persuade people by *logos*, but rather offers a suggestion to them by showing them a path. And this act of "showing the path" is repeated, reproduced, and expanded through *mimesis* and cultural transmission.

---

19. McFague, *Blessed Are the Consumers*, 152. The latter quotation is actually Rohr's words.
20. McFague, *Blessed Are the Consumers*, 152.
21. McFague, *Blessed Are the Consumers*, 33.

PART I. KENOSIS IN POLITICAL THEOLOGY

Is there potential for interreligious dialogue in this approach? The Kyoto School, in the broad sense, represents a precedent for engaging with the word "kenosis" and thus opening the possibility for interreligious dialogue. The Kyoto School was a group of intellectuals consisting of Kitaro Nishida and his students and colleagues who were at the forefront of Japanese philosophy in the first half of the twentieth century. In the background of their intellectual development were their reflections on the rapid and drastic transformations that Japan encountered during the realization of Western-style modernization from the Meiji period onwards. Some central questions for the Kyoto School, thus, were the following: "What does the modernization of Japan, as a non-Western country, mean to the people living there?" "Did this radical change bring an unconquerable disease of Nihilism along with material prosperity?" Importantly, the members of the Kyoto School did not adopt a merely anti-modernist or reactionary conservative stance. Instead, they investigated the occidental metaphysics and Christianity that lay at the root of Western culture and developed a new way of thinking, which I call an "art of translation," to reconcile them with their own traditions, such as Buddhism.

In particular, they focused on kenosis in their efforts to create a new philosophy of religion. Kitaro Nishida, in his final article "The Logic of Place [*Basho*] and the Religious Worldview," which he wrote at the end of his life and during the final days of World War II, states:

> A God who is simply self-sufficient in a transcendent way is not the true God. It must have a kenotic aspect that is everywhere present. A truly dialectic God will be one that is at all times transcendent as it is immanent and immanent as it is transcendent. This is what makes a true absolute. It is said that God created the world out of love. Then God's absolute love has to be something essential to God as an absolute self-negation, not as an opus ad extra.[22]

I will not analyze this passage in detail here. What is important is that, as Tobias Bartneck notes, Nishida's successors (Tanabe, Nishitani, Abe, and others) drew inspiration from this passage and attempted to build their own religious philosophies.[23] Odin refers to this interpretive strategy (that

---

22. Heisig, *Philosophers of Nothingness*, 102, quoting Nishida Zenshu. See also Bartneck, "Kenosis," 203.

23. Bartneck, "Kenosis."

is, a new interpretation of Christianity from a Buddhist standpoint) as "Japanese kenoticism."[24]

My own exploration of the term "kenosis" might be understood more or less as a continuation of the Kyoto School's "Japanese kenoticism." However, it is not easy to say whether the "path" of non-naturalistic universalization through "metaphorical thinking" that I have indicated above is similar to their attempts. In any case, however, what is important for our attempt is that kenosis is not a metaphysical entity or operative principle exclusive to Christianity. Rather, it is, perhaps, the very "between" that allows for the intersection and resonance of various ideas and concepts. It is not a specific realm, but an *empty source* from which new experiences and realities emerge as possibilities.[25]

5. TENTATIVE CONCLUSION

In this chapter, I have focused on kenosis as a new universal life-form for surviving the current polycrisis. I took up McFague's kenotic theology as a pioneering framework in this approach. In a manner that echoes Taylor and Butler, she thoroughly critiques the individualistic model of human life that has been dominant since the eighteenth century. Instead, she proposes a new model of life based on interdependence—the kenotic model.

The most ambitious parts of McFague's work lie in her claims that this kenotic model or "spirituality of subtraction" is (1) scientifically provable and (2) present to some degree in every religion. Both of these two are universalizations of kenosis. Regarding (1), she pays particular attention to the natural phenomenon of "nurse logs." Here, old trees negate their own existence and give way to others, enabling a symbiotic relationship among trees. Furthermore, following Churchland, she argues that there is a natural scientific basis for the care ethic of humans rooted in the cooperative nature of mammalians and their instinctive love for their offspring. I refer to this Churchland-McFague's strategy as "naturalizing kenosis." In today's world, where the divide between science and religion continues to grow, such a bold approach is to some degree commendable. However, I refrain from making an immediate judgment on this aspect of her work. At the

---

24. Odin, "Critique of '*Kenōsis/Śūnyatā*' Motif."

25. In this, I refer to what Niels Weidtmann means by the word "between [*das Zwischen*]" as a key concept for intercultural philosophy (Weidtmann, *Interkulturelle Philosophie*, 180).

same time, I also suspend the possibility of dialogue between science and religion through kenotic ethics.

Instead, I find greater potential in her second claim (2). The key lies in understanding kenosis metaphorically rather than strictly as a doctrine or concept. While McFague herself does not explicitly distinguish between naturalizing and metaphorical thinking, I would argue that metaphorical thinking is useful for the universalization of kenosis. Just as Jesus does kenosis, Buddha does self-emptying; just as Daoists respect Wu-Wei, Christians respect kenosis. It is possible that these associations, drawn through the analogy of "as," offer another possibility for universalization—one that might also open avenues for dialogue with science.

While *naturalism* presupposes a metaphysical framework that governs all things and events, *metaphorical thinking*, which lacks this kind of metaphysical background, drives each subject to associate and translate ideas across various contexts. The former aims for sameness, while the latter emphasizes *similarity*. Is it possible for this constant processual translation to lead to a universal life-form? That question is what I would attempt to explore through the process of interreligious or intercultural philosophy. Moreover, such an approach would align with McFague's vision: "A kenotic theology must be reconstructed for each new age and set of circumstances. . . . One religion, Christianity, might contribute to addressing the crucial issues of our time. . . . Because theology is necessarily and always metaphorical."[26]

BIBLIOGRAPHY

Bartneck, Tobias. "Kenosis Seen from the Standpoint of Nishitani Keiji: Towards a New Understanding of the Kyoto School's Interpretation of Christianity." 求真 28 (2023) 199–213.
Bubbio, Paolo Diego. *Sacrifice in the Post-Kantian Tradition: Perspectivism, Intersubjectivity, and Recognition*. Contemporary Continental Philosophy. New York: SUNY Press, 2014.
Butler, Judith. *The Force of Nonviolence: An Ethico-Political Bind*. London: Verso, 2020.
Churchland, Patricia S. *Braintrust: What Neuroscience Tells Us about Morality*. Princeton Science Library. Princeton, NJ: Princeton University Press, 2011.
Heisig, James W. *Philosophers of Nothingness: An Essay on the Kyoto School*. Nanzan Library of Asian Religion and Culture. Honolulu: University of Hawaii Press, 2001.
Latour, Bruno. *We Have Never Been Modern*. Translated by Catherine Porter. Cambridge, MA: Harvard University Press, 1993.

---

26. McFague, *Blessed Are the Consumers*, 174.

McFague, Sallie. *Blessed Are the Consumers: Climate Change and the Practice of Restraint.* Minneapolis: Fortress, 2013.

———. *A New Climate for Christianity: Kenosis, Climate Change, and Befriending Nature.* Minneapolis: Fortress, 2021.

Odin, Steve. "A Critique of the '*Kenōsis/Śūnyatā*' Motif in Nishida and the Kyoto School." *Buddhist-Christian Studies* 9 (1989) 71–86.

Parvaiz, Athar. "Scientists in India Protest Move to Drop Darwinian Evolution from Textbooks." *Science*, Apr. 28, 2023. https://www.science.org/content/article/scientists-india-protest-move-drop-darwinian-evolution-textbooks.

Sloterdijk, Peter. *Du musst dein Leben ändern: On Human Engineering.* Berlin: Suhrkamp, 2009.

Taylor, Charles. *A Secular Age.* Cambridge, MA: Harvard University Press, 2007.

Weidtmann, Niels. *Interkulturelle Philosophie: Aufgaben—Dimensionen—Wege.* Tübingen: Francke, 2016.

2

Kenosis
Towards a Political Theology of Love

Saitya Brata Das

THE ENIGMA OF KENOSIS

> For I have already told you that suffering and sorrow increase in proportion to love: when love grows, so does sorrow.
> —Catherine of Siena[1]

What follows is a reflection—of a theologico-political nature—on what is at stake in this word "kenosis" (with certain grammatical modification) which occurs in Saint Paul's letters.[2] Most decisive moment of this idea manifests itself in Paul's Letter to the Philippians wherein he writes:

> [Christ Jesus] who, being in the form of God, thought it not robbery to be equal with God: but *emptied himself*, and took upon him the

---

1. *Dialogue*, 33.
2. In what follows I will keep to absolute minimum references to the vast body of secondary literature that exists and continues to grow around this key idea of Paul: what is important for me here is not so much to provide a scholarly discussion of this idea—for which numberless works exist—but to make manifest a moment, essential to this profound idea, by an attentive reading of Paul's letter in its spirit, as much as it is possible for me.

form of a servant, and was made in the likeness of man: and being found in fashion as a man, he humbled himself, and became obedient unto death, even the death on the cross. (Phil 2:6–8)[3]

Scholars and philosophers like Stanislas Breton locate in Isaiah's "suffering servant" (Isa 52:14; 53:1–6) Paul's inspiration for his *doulos Christou*.[4] To make oneself "in the likeness of man" is to suffer in the obedience that this *analogia* itself demands, which is obedience "unto death, even the death on the cross." This *analogia*, this *likeness*, is not the *analogia* of that which constitutes the force of being of these two beings—the divine and the human: it is not the question here of the sovereign force of the divine being meeting up, at a sovereign instance of encounter, the force of the being called "man," and thereby neutralizing the hiatus between the mortality of the one and glory of the other;[5] rather, it is precisely the question here of assuming the form of nothing, which barely is a form, let alone a figure—that of a slave, a servant, a nothing indeed. To take upon—that is, vicariously (we cannot miss the vicarious mode of "taking upon")—this formless form, this figureless figure, this disfigured face of someone who is no one is to empty oneself unto this no one who is now hanging on the cross, his eyes vacant, his blood oozing out of his wounds. The whole letter is nothing other than an invitation to the Philippians: come and participate in this kenosis of God; may our own emptying—of the force of being—analogically meet up this divine emptying so that we learn to live our life without force, for that alone is redemptive. What else does *redemption* mean if not to live without the elemental forces that coerce us today? Is *redemption* anything else apart from living without those ties (political, religious, ethnic etc) that bind us to the *nomos* of the worldly order," to live without the normative obligations to the existing forces of the world that are represented in "all principality, and power, and might" (Eph 1:21–23) so that we can be free for God through him who is hanging on the cross now? What else is life

---

3. Scripture quotations in this chapter are from the KJV.

4. Breton: *Radical Philosophy of Saint Paul*; *Word and the Cross*.

5. Thus, even so resolute a thinker of analogy like Hans Urs von Balthasar has this to say: "On the other hand, the tracklessness (*aporia*) which confronts us like a yawning abyss in the hiatus of the death of man and of God must at all costs be preserved from the attempt to render it innocuous through an intellectually comprehensible 'analogy' between the before and the after, the mortal Jesus and the risen kyrios, earth and heaven. The 'stumbling block of the cross' must not be 'removed' (Galatians 5:11); the 'cross of Christ' must not be 'emptied of its power' (1 Corinthians 1:17)" (Balthasar, *Mysterium Paschale*, 52).

other than life redeemed? For the redeemed life alone is the life truly alive. But to participate in this glorious life of blessedness, first we must undergo this empty measure of time, the time of the night—on the cross; we must *pass* through the empty *passage*—this kenotic passage—where, denuded of all the adjectives of the human tongue we are exposed to the desert of attributes;[6] we must untie those ties that otherwise bind us to the nomos of the worldly order. This is the invitation that Paul sends to the Philippians—the invitation to take up the cross and follow him who already has gone ahead by emptying himself on the cross. This is a costly invitation, not only because the inviter himself has to kenotically give up everything on this cross (and already the Lord has gone by ahead of us, he who by emptying himself becomes an impossible example, for he left us a measure which is impossible for us to measure) but also because those who are invited are to empty themselves—so that the beloved becomes *like* the lover, the disciple becomes *like* the teacher in an *analogy* of love. God's kenosis gratuitously pours forth a measureless gift—unequal and unsaturated in the worldly economy of all worldly values—but it is no cheap gift that can be bought at bargain prices in the marketplace of the world; it is costly grace, as someone like Dietrich Bonhoeffer would put it:[7] we must take up, each one of us, in solitude and yet together, the form of the nothing that God himself has come to take up. Now this immense cost, this prodigious dying to the world and emptying, is scandalous and foolishness by the measure of worldly wisdom. In one of his beautiful edifying discourses and in many other places too, Søren Kierkegaard dwells on this, and brings out for us the essential message—the stakes, the risk, the wager of love that exceeds the economy of the worldly values:

> To *follow Christ* means to take up one's cross or, as it says in the text just read, to carry one's cross. To carry one's cross means to deny oneself, as Christ explains it when he says, "if anyone would

---

6. "Desert" is the favorite term for Meister Eckhart: desert is the non-place and non-time, devoid of all why, where God's emptying out pours itself onto man: desert "being" that non-place where all address and all tracks, all whereto and all wherefrom, get lost. In one of his sermons Eckhart says: "I say the same thing about the man who has brought himself to naught in himself and in God and in all creatures: that man has assumed the lowest place, and God is bound to empty Himself totally into him, or He would not be God" (*Complete Mystical Works*, 309). Eckhart's fundamental teaching of *Gelazenheit* (contemporary Germ.: *Gelassenheit*) understands kenosis as abandonment, but also as birth: God's emptying pouring onto man is at once the birth of the soul in God and God's birthing himself in the soul.

7. Bonhoeffer, *Cost of Discipleship*.

come after me, let him deny himself and take up his cross and follow me" (Matthew 16:24). It was also "this mind that was in Christ Jesus, he who thought it not robbery to be equal to God but humbled himself and became obedient unto death, even to death on the cross" (Philippians 2:5ff). As was the prototype, so must the imitation also be, even though it is a *slow and difficult task* to deny oneself, a heavy cross to take up, a heavy cross to bear, and one that, according to the prototype's instructions, is to be carried in obedience unto death, so that the imitator, even if he does not die on the cross, nevertheless resembles the prototype in dying "with the cross on."[8]

It is interesting that Kierkegaard reads together these two passages—Matt 16:24, which Dietrich Bonhoeffer's justly famous book on discipleship reflects upon, and the passage on kenosis from Phil 2:7. And it is illuminating for us to read together Bonhoeffer's thought on costly discipleship with Kierkegaard's gospel of suffering: they bear upon the *theologia crucis*,[9] so crucial for Luther, that puts into question all triumphalism in advance by insisting on the scandalous and foolish event of revelation which, for each one of these thinkers, is revelation of God's very no-thing and nonbeing. Kierkegaard's "Gospel of Sufferings"—one of the edifying discourses by that name from which the above lines are cited—underlines this messianic paradox of the gospel by concentrating itself on the cross with a singular attention: "gospel" (that is, "good news," *God-spell*, which attempts to render into English the Roman *evangelium* and the Greek *Euangelion*) and "suffering" are brought together in a paradoxical coincidence of the incommensurable which is offensive to the wisdom of the world and a scandal for those zealous for the law. There cannot simply be a "gospel of suffering," a "good news of suffering"; such a thing goes against the very truth of the world. Yet for Kierkegaard this is precisely what "gospel" means in the true sense of the word. Here for Kierkegaard—as for Paul's paradoxical formulation of "hope against hope" (Rom 4:18)—the paradox here is not a mere rhetorical strategy; it is the very truth of revelation: hope which can be hoped for, the hope that is grounded upon the presently available facts of the world which can be grasped by knowledge is not truly hope, for the true and unconditional hope must open the horizon of existence beyond the given state of affairs of the world, beyond what can be hoped for; likewise the true gospel is not the gospel of what has already triumphantly arrived in the

8. Kierkegaard, "Gospel of Sufferings," 221; emphasis in original.
9. For contemporary renewal of this thought, see Moltmann, *Crucified God*.

world but that which must infinitely, in a qualitative sense, open the world to that what the world has never experienced itself on the basis of its own possibility—that is the gospel in the true sense. What the gospel announces and makes us glad is not the truth of the world as it exists but that beatitude or blessedness that can only be undergone, here and now, as suffering, and hence can only be for human understanding and for the human wisdom a *para-doxa*: the cross is paradox—at once invoking vicarious suffering, and in suffering, it immediately, here and now, joyfully announcing the redemption of the world. The gospel of suffering thus, for Kierkegaard—like the gospel of Paul's "hope against hope"—is not still another, new gospel; rather all gospels of the New Testament are *gospel* in this essential sense: that it affirms the unconditional against the economy of the world as it exists, and as such, this gospel can appear in the unredeemed world only by bearing the question mark which *crosses out* the *wisdom* and the *law* of the world. What *wisdom* calls *foolishness*, the *law* calls *scandal*: an offense or an ignominy unlovable, yet precisely to be loved so that love overcomes the offense and ignominy of the unlovable, so that love—like hope—comes to love the unlovable, which alone is love unconditional and redemptive. The paradox here—both Paul's and Kierkegaard's—points to a truth which cannot be verified as the truth of the world, for it exceeds what exists as "truth" in the world: the paradox here is not a mere rhetorical strategy of language; it is an index which is of messianic nature—it opens up the truth of the world to that which the world has *not* yet come to see.

The true gospel, then, is the gospel of the cross and is the gospel of suffering—only then, once the dark rays of the gospel passes and pierces through the abyss of the night—the night when the abyss invokes the abyss[10]—only then will there diffuse the radiant glory of Christ, as Paul would say in the very next lines to the Philippians, after he has spoken of God's kenosis and of the imperative for those who follow Christ to empty themselves on the cross by taking up the cross: "Therefore God also has highly exalted Him and given Him the name which is above every name" (Phil 2:9). Thus kenosis and glory are inseparable: God's emptying in his self-revelation points towards, eschatologically, to his own glory. In fact, Kierkegaard would go onto say, in his incomparable contemplation of kenosis, that for us who are here and now, as it was for the apostles, kenosis itself is glorious: that is the meaning of Matt 16:24. Only thus suffering itself is turned into good news and the gospel becomes truly gospel—that is, the

---

10. "Abyssus abyssum invocat" (Ps 42:7).

gospel of suffering. Kierkegaard's attentive ears don't fail to listen what is spoken of the apostles in the Acts: "And to him they agreed: and when they had called the apostles, and beaten them, they commanded that they should not speak in the name of Jesus, and let them go. So they departed from the presence of the council, rejoicing that they were counted worthy to suffer shame for His name" (Acts 5:40–41).

Here is, then—in Bonhoeffer as much as in Kierkegaard, both following Pauline paradoxical messianic logic of kenosis—God's kenosis calls for the kenosis on the part of the disciples who follow Christ. This, then, is the *analogia* between what, in accordance to the wisdom of the world, is scandalously incongruous and foolish to the point of absurdity: God made himself a *likeness* to men so that men may in turn *resemble* God; God *empties* himself on the cross in becoming human so that the human in turn may *empty* himself on the cross; God becomes—out of the abyss of divine love—other than who he is (and therein lies his suffering), so that the human may participate in that which is radically otherwise than its possibility and capacity. This opening of the human beyond its capacity and possibility can only be a gratuitous gift of freedom out of an abyss of love where the incalculable metamorphosis can happen: suffering itself can become gospel in turn; kenosis itself can become glorious for the apostles and for the disciples who have taken up the cross and are obedient unto death.

In parenthesis: It is this offensive paradox of the early Christianity as underlined by Paul in his kenosis passage and in other places that is renounced by the triumphant Christendom of Kierkegaard's time, which is ours too: truth that is originally a scandal and foolishness and offensive to the world has now sought to be transformed into the truth and the law of the world: this is Kierkegaard's point, following the Paul who in his own time puts into question—by bringing up the offensive question of kenosis—the truth and the law of the world, the Paul who tries to open up life enclosed within the regime of the law to a new, true life, which is found in *ecclesia*, which is a community neither grounded on ethnic-biological ties of the natural men nor on the normative obligations to the existing political hegemonies in the world. It is the merit of Jacob Taubes to bring out this moment in Paul in his careful reading of the Letter to the Romans, thereby polemically responding to Schmitt's decisionist political theology of sovereignty.[11] Important for us will be to read a particular passage from Paul to be able to bring out what is at stake here—the passage of Rom 9–11—where

11. Taubes, *Political Theology of Paul*.

the word "enemy" occurs, the crucial point of contention between Taubes and Schmitt. We will briefly discuss it once again. But before that we will have to come back to the Paul's kenosis passage, which is what we are discussing here and now.

To come back to Paul's Letter to the Philippians: What, then, is this passage saying? Kenosis "is" the empty measure of space and empty measure of time—and yet full, precisely thereby, abundantly abounding, the very fullness of time, dense with presence that revelation lends to it, dense with the dazzling darkness of the divine light as Pseudo-Dionysus would like to say:[12] the meeting point between the divine and the mortal is the empty space and empty time where the world, having been emptied of the force of its law, may resemble the one who is dying on the cross, emptied of the divine force, denuded of the divine *potentia*. The event of revelation is, then, the very mystery of suffering which is grounded on the abyss of divine love. This enigma of kenosis lets itself be thought, itself a radical gift—outside our ability and capacity—only in this incomprehensible unity of suffering and love. In the mystery of suffering lies the very gift of love: where there is no love, suffering is not redeeming.

What, then, is love? To put it simply, love is that which opens me beyond myself, in an excentric and ex-tatic movement of *excessus*: God's love too is the excentric movement of suspending the judgment of God's law. Where there is love, judgment is suspended: the suspension of judgment, then, is the very possibility of love. This is how Paul's messianic logic can bring a radical dissymmetry between the nomos, which finds its articulation in the dictation of the law, and, on the other hand, the abyss of agape that must precede all judgment as if in an immemorial fashion. The immemorial abyss of agape—love that opens up the gap and exposes open the empty space of time so that the incommensurables are brought together and are redeemed—precedes the work of the law: in the chasm of love, the work of nomos becomes inoperative. By a freedom of love, which is love's decision, God excentrically and ex-tactically empties himself into the form which is barely that of being, let alone a figure it is: the non-thing of the slave, dying ignominious and scandalous death on the cross. On that cross God lets his own potentia go and lets himself suffer—out of the abyss of his love. This kenotic event of revelation out of the freedom of love frees God himself as if as it were from himself: he *weakens* himself, and makes himself this "extra-divine logos"—as Schelling was to ecstatically interpret this kenosis

---

12. Pseudo-Dionysus, "Mystical Theology," 135.

of God[13]—so that the world, which is groaning for redemption until now, as Paul says,[14] becomes redeemed from the force of the law that coerces it. The point I am making here is none other than this: Paul's critique of the law—of this nomos of the earth—cannot be understood without what Paul calls as *love* whose mystery is at once is the mystery of suffering whose prodigious unity is condensed to an extreme degree in this one word that occurs in this letter: the word is none other than "kenosis." Herein lies the question of God's self-revelation itself which is nothing other than revelation of love that has to manifest—in a fashion which is the very paradox of Paul's messianism—in suffering, as suffering: God's emptying on the cross. With this the claim of autochthony and sovereignty on the part of world-political powers—of "all principality, and power and might"—is rendered transient, having only the sense of eschatological provisionality: "For the fashion of this world passeth away" (1 Cor 7:31). The world-political powers lose the sense of ultimacy and sovereignty in this eschatological light: the essence of their existence is to pass away.

SCANDAL AND FOOLISHNESS

Thus, the cross is already a scandal and foolishness, as Paul writes to the Corinthians (1 Cor 1:23); however, an invitation to participate in this scandalous foolishness, or in this foolish scandal, is also equally foolish and scandalous. Living in a world that has remarkably been changed in the 2,000 years from the time Paul wrote these words, we perhaps cannot imagine the foolishness and scandalous character of this Pauline invitation, but in Paul's own time it must have been really scandalous. In the last polemical writings just before his death, Kierkegaard's scandalous critique of what he calls "Christendom"—as opposed to "Christianity"—seeks to renew this

---

13. "The true God is the living God," writes Schelling, "living means to dispose of one's Being freely; the living God goes beyond himself by his own power and becomes something Other than his unforethinkable Being, different from the Being in which he is *a se* [by himself]" (*Philosophy of Revelation*, 137; emphasis in original). Schelling then goes on to speak of this kenosis, which is the very mark of God as living: "God does not empty himself into the world. Rather, he elevates himself with his Godhead; he is emptied of himself unforethinkably. He goes within himself by suspending the *actus*. At the same time, God suspends the *actus* of his necessary existence to posit a Being other than his own in place of his first existence" (146).

14. "For we know that the whole creation groaneth and travaileth in pain together until now" (Rom 8:22).

scandal and this foolishness once again, the scandal and foolishness that the 1,800 years of Christendom is happy to renounce: Christendom makes the virtue of this renunciation in a triumphalism by incorporating itself into the world-historical politics. That the church officials of Denmark found this Kierkegaard's final critique of Christendom scandalous is precisely what he sought out, for the originary spirit of Christianity for him is not the triumphalism and the apology for the world as it exists but *kenotic* emptying out of the attributes of the worldly nomos. For Paul, and for Kierkegaard too who scandalously attempts to renew Christianity's originary scandalous spirit (which is to be carried out *existentially* in the transfiguration of his life as this singular individual) kenosis has nothing to do with triumphalism of any world-historical-political powers; if there is glory, that too is Christ's, that is an eschatological—though imminent—event; while hic et nunc for us this glory can manifest itself, paradoxically—that is, offensively—only as suffering which points towards, in an oblique manner—without thereby doing away with God's radical invisibility—as the abyss of God's incomprehensible love.

We are thus trying to understand why the cross—or, better to say, why does the crucified God—appears to be so scandalous and foolish. The obvious answer is: the cross reveals the abyss, the night, the emptiness in God himself. No doubt that Saint John of the Cross, the doctor of mystical life (the doctor who bears the cross in his very name and carries the cross in his very life) would call one of his books *The Dark Night of the Soul*. What the event of revelation reveals—as the event of God's self-revelation, an infinitely unsaturated event that it is—is nothing other than nothing, the no one and no-thing in God himself, the dark night of God where God's own potentiality comes to be impotential and becomes invisible in turn. The event of revelation is at once an *incognitus* (this is the word that Kierkegaard also likes to use): this paradox is the very enigma of kenosis, that God's revelation reveals as much as conceals—in and through his very self-revelation. God reveals himself in a "form"—barely a "form" it is, let alone being a "figure" (all these words need to be used within double quotation marks)—the form of no one, in the form which he himself is not, in the form in which the thing is not, a non-thing. What is this form which is the form of no-thing? Or, perhaps to put it better: Who is this form which is the form of no one? Paul the Roman—who nevertheless writes in Greek, who as a Jew had tremendous zeal for the law of the ancestors—answers: He is the slave. It is the slave who is no one, barely a thing, almost no figure, hardly a form: the minimal that it is possible to reduce oneself to, that minimal possible so that this bare light renders this no one visible in whose visibility the invisible can un-reveal himself through this event of self-revelation. This is the paradox that Paul grapples with, and it is this same paradox that comes to haunt, after 1,800 years, that singular individual called Søren Kierkegaard who comes to untie all the ties that normatively bind him to the nomos of the world to win an ever new freedom by losing everything by becoming no-thing. This is the messianic logic of redemption, both Paul's and Kierkegaard's, the logic whose paradox appears more illogical than logical to the wise Greeks: for them it is foolishness; in the eyes of the wisdom of the world it is absolutely ignominious; and for Nietzsche the antichrist—who rediscovers the tragic wisdom of the Greeks towards the completion of two millennia of Christendom—it is sheer idiocy. For those who are zealous for the law, the cross is the incomparable scandal. Thus theologians and historians of religion like Martin Hengel demonstrate with rigorous scholarly exegesis how ignominious the cross was for the ancient world and still is, the cross that puts a question mark to all that is triumphant in the worldly order of nomos (of "all principality, and power, and might").[15] This is the paradox of kenosis: that God (who is the Lord of all that exists, as actual and possible for him) reveals himself as nothing; that this unique and only once happened event of revelation reveals rather the emptiness of his being, the vacancy of the divine power, the withdrawal of his divine force—and not the force of his Being. This divine kenosis calls forth the kenosis from us so that we can become the *likeness* of God, like a beloved who becomes *like* the lover, and becoming this *likeness*, we may receive what exceeds human capacity and possibility (which renders the autochthony of the human and of all that is human, all its "principality, and power and might," provisional and transient). This event of God emptying of himself thereby also reveals—not as ad-extra but intrinsically—solidarity with those who are oppressed and vanquished by the nomos of world-sovereign powers. The form of nonbeing—that of the suffering servant which God vicariously takes up—does not use the world as something to be used up and to be abused; and those who follow the suffering servant are *alike* to this suffering servant: they "use this world, as not abusing it" (1 Cor 7:31). Living as it were in the time of the end, at the end of time, they are in the world as if they are already not, as if already are they stepping beyond: "those who weep as though they did not weep, those who rejoice as though

---

15. Hengel, *Crucifixion*.

they did not rejoice, those who buy as though they did not possess" (1 Cor 7:30). With this kenosis, the *oikonomia* of the worldly possessions—with its logic of equivalences of values—is emptied out of the fullness of its force and are transvalued. The worldly economy of values is now exposed open to that which is unconditionally uneconomic: the redemptive gift of joy without measure and calculation. The sorrowful face of the slave, that of the suffering servant, is united thus with the most profound joy, rendering the gospel truly the gospel of suffering. In Paul, love has no other meaning that this kenotic sense of servicing the world, the unconditional and self-effacing service that can't be reducible to any calculable and conditioned negotiations of political-economic programs. Like Kierkegaard's "gospel of suffering" Stanislas Breton could thus speak of the paradoxical unity of joy and suffering on the cross: "Seen from the height of the cross, the problem of the world changes its meaning: more than using it, the essential thing is to serve it. Now the 'unconditional service' for which Christ furnishes the model unites, in a single freedom, the forgetting of self, signified for us by 'kenosis,' not to speak of that oblation without reserve that grants to the servant the limitless space of possible transformations . . . the void or 'hollowing out' only 'mortifies' so that the individual empirical sphere might be opened to a broader horizon. . . . But this sacrifice, in a new paradox, unites suffering with the most profound joy: that of a gift given without reserve or calculation."[16]

INFINITE LOVE

To sum it up, what I attempted is to show that under the exodus of God in kenosis, the mystery of love coincides with the ineffable night of divine suffering. This calls forth a loving response on the part of those who take up the cross and follow Christ to form the covenant which cannot be understood on the basis of the normative ties—ethnic as much as political—that bind us to the hegemonic forces of the world. This call is a call to undo the oppositional symmetry that constitutes the law of the world. This is why the call necessarily assumes the form of a paradoxical imperative: hope against hope, love the unlovable, and love the enemy. By confounding the wisdom of the world, such a call transforms the nothing into everything, and lends to those with no-face or disfigured face—of the disinherited ones, vanquished by the law of the world, oppressed of every kind—the dignity of a

16. Breton, *Radical Philosophy of Saint Paul*, 153.

face: suffering turning into a gospel. For this sake the divine himself vicariously pours into the nothing of kenosis—out of a love that freely disposes his own Being on the cross.

The cross thus confounds the logic of symmetry that constitutes the regime of phenomena of the world. In his deconstructive reading of Carl Schmitt, Jacques Derrida goes onto undo—after a thoughtful meditation on Kierkegaard—this oppositional symmetry of friend and enemy which constitutes Schmitt's concept of the political.[17] For what Schmitt seeks, by an appeal to Paul, the legitimacy of world sovereign power on a theological foundation. But such an attempt comes to a point of aporia when one comes to the paradoxical demand of love: "love your enemy," which undoes the oppositional logic of symmetry. At stake here is a crucial passage from Paul—Rom 9–11—where the concept of enemy occurs, the passage the exegesis of which is also the point of contention between Taubes and Schmitt. The reading of this passage must attend not only to the delicate distinction drawn between *hostis* and *inimicus* but also that the word "loved" occurs in the very next verse. Taubes thus writes to Schmitt: "The word 'enemy' also appears there, in the absolute sense, but—this seems to me to be the most decisive of decisive points—connected with 'loved.'"[18] Taubes further writes: "And now comes this powerful sentence about which I deliberated with Carl Schmitt . . . : 'as regards the gospel they are enemies'—enemies of God! Enemy is not a private concept; enemy is *hostis*, not *inimicus*, that's

---

17. Derrida thus writes "to remind us of the remark made by Carl Schmitt when, in chapter 3 of *The Concept of the Political*, he emphasizes that fact that *inimicus* is not *hostis* in Latin and *ekhthros* is not *polemios* in Greek. This allows him to conclude that Christ's teaching concerns the love that we just show to our private enemies, to those we would be tempted to hate through personal or subjective passion, and not to public enemies. . . . Christ's teaching would thus be moral or psychological, even metaphysical, but not political. This is important for Schmitt, for whom war waged against a determinate enemy (*hostis*), a war or hostility that does not presuppose hate, would be condition of possibility of politics" (*Gift of Death*, 103). Derrida then goes on to say: "Among other things this raises again the question of a Christian politics, one that conforms to the Gospels. For Schmitt, but in a very different sense from Patôcka, a Christian or European Christian politics seems possible. The modern sense of the political itself would be tied to such a possibility inasmuch as political concepts are secularized theologico-political concepts. But for that to make sense one must presuppose that Schmitt's reading of 'love your enemy' pre-empts all discussion, or we might say, all ethico-philological debate, since the war waged against the Muslims, to cite but a single case, was a political fact, in Schmitt's sense, and it confirmed that existence of a Christian politics, of a coherent intention of bringing all Christians and the whole church together in a spirit of consensus" (103–4).

18. Taubes, *Political Theology of Paul*, 113.

not my enemy. When it says: 'Love your enemy'—yes, perhaps, I'm not sure what it means there in the Sermon on the Mount. Here, in any case, we are not dealing with private feuds, but with salvation—historical enemies of God. 'Enemies for your sake; but as regards election they are beloved, for the sake of their forefathers' (Rom 11:28). This is the point I challenged Schmitt on, that he does not see this dialectic that moves Paul and that the Christian church after 70 has forgotten, that he adopted not a text but a tradition, that is the folk traditions of church antisemitism, onto which he, in 1933–36, in his uninhibited fashion, went onto graft the racist theozoology."[19]

In the form of the cross, Christ kenotically brings together, at an absolute abyssal point of nothing, suffering and love without which there is no redemption. This kenotic love thereby releases earthly existence from the ontological violence of force against force, from the mythical violence of the eternal return of power. The cross of God undoes the oppositional symmetry of force against force which constitutes the sovereign powers of world-historical politics; and the divine undoes it by an infirmity which is at once a scandal and foolishness. This demands—and this has already been thought through by Schelling—that we think of the mystery of love once again as inseparable from the mystery of suffering, love as the very ground of existence. This is so insofar as this love is so free that it loves even the unlovable: thus love lovingly undoes the oppositional symmetry of the worldly nomos. Only in the light of this divine love all earthly suffering can be absorbed, transfigured and redeemed. In a letter written after Caroline's death, Schelling thus writes: "I now need friends who are not strangers to the real seriousness of pain and who feel that the single right and happy state of the soul is the divine mourning in which all earthly pain is immersed."[20] Only such divine love knows, in its deepest depth, the abyss of suffering and thereby can transfigure and redeem it. To participate in this abyss of divine love—which is at once the divine sorrow—the triumphalism of the worldly order is at once humbled and transcended. It is the

---

19. Taubes, *Political Theology of Paul*, 51.

20. Schelling, "Brief über den Tod Carolines." In another instance Schelling writes of this infinite abandonment as the very kenotic task of philosophizing and existing: "He who wishes to place himself in the beginning of a truly free philosophy must abandon even God. Here we say: who wishes to maintain it, he will lose it; and who gives it up, he will find it. Only he has come to the ground of himself and has known the whole depth of life who has once abandoned everything and has himself been abandoned by everything. He for whom everything disappeared and who saw himself alone with the infinite: a great step which Plato compared to death" (quoted in Heidegger, *Schelling's Treatise*, 6–7).

same kenotic movement which pours itself in incarnation and in crucifixion, thereby opening the world to the eschatological glory of redemption. This kenotic tonality which attunes the whole earthly order of existence in its transiency cannot be understood *kathekontically* as it is sought to be interpreted by political theologians like Carl Schmitt.[21] This is insofar as the cross stands as question mark—as love's judgment, not that of the law—over all the worldly hegemonies in place. This abyssal love, in its very fragility, has precisely thereby bears a "power" to redeem the suffering of the oppressed humanity along with nature. In becoming nothing, it transforms the nothing into a name that is above all names. Today's political theology has no other task than this very task of thinking redemption which will stand like a star to guide the darkness of the world to that light where all time is permeated by the dazzling darkness of eternity.

BIBLIOGRAPHY

Balthasar, Hans Urs von. *Mysterium Paschale*. Translated by Aidan Nichols. San Francisco: Ignatius, 2000.
Bonhoeffer, Dietrich. *The Cost of Discipleship*. Translated by R. H. Fuller. New York: Touchstone, 1995.
Breton, Stanislas. *A Radical Philosophy of Saint Paul*. Translated by Joseph Ballan. New York: Columbia University Press, 2011.
———. *The Word and The Cross*. Translated by Jacquelyn Porter. Fordham: Fordham University Press, 2002.
Catherine of Siena. *The Dialogue*. Translated by Suzanne Noffke. New York: Paulist, 1980.
Derrida, Jacques. *The Gift of Death*. Translated by David Wills. Chicago: Chicago University Press, 1995.
Eckhart, Meister. *The Complete Mystical Works*. Translated by Maurice Walshe. New York: Crossroad, 2009.
Heidegger, Martin. *Schelling's Treatise on the Essence of Human Freedom*. Translated by Joan Stambaugh. Athens: Ohio University Press, 1985.
Hengel, Martin. *Crucifixion: In the Ancient World and Folly of the Message of the Cross*. Translated by John Bowden. Philadelphia: Fortress, 1977.
John of the Cross. *The Dark Night of the Soul*. Edited by Halcyon Backhouse. London: Holder, 2009.
Kierkegaard, Søren. "The Gospel of Sufferings." In *Upbuilding Discourses in Various Spirits*, edited and translated by Howard V. Hong and Edna H. Hong, 213–342. Kierkegaard's Writings 15. Princeton, NJ: Princeton University Press, 1993.
Moltmann, Jürgen. *The Crucified God*. Translated by A. A Wilson and John Bowden. Minneapolis: Fortress, 1993.
Pseudo-Dionysus. "The Mystical Theology." In *The Complete Works*, translated by Colm Luibheid, 133–42. New York: Paulist, 1987.

21. Schmitt, *Nomos of the Earth*.

Schelling, F. W. J. von. "Brief über den Tod Carolines vom 2. Oktober, 1809." In *Kleine Kommentierte Texte 1*, edited by Johann Ludwig Döderlein. Stuttgart-Bad Cannstatt, Germ.: Frommann-Holzboog, 1975.

———. *Philosophy of Revelation*. Translated by Klaus Ottmann. Putnam, CT: Thompson, 2020.

Schmitt, Carl. *The Nomos of the Earth in the International Law of Jus Publicum Europaeum*. Translated by G. L. Ulmen. New York: Telos, 2006.

Taubes, Jacob. *The Political Theology of Paul*. Translated by Dana Hollander. Cultural Memory in the Present. Stanford, CA: Stanford University Press, 2004.

3

Mystici Corpori
From the Kenotic Christ to the Kenotic Church—Fragments of a Grand Narrative[*]

TOBIAS BARTNECK

> For our God is a consuming fire.
> —HEB 12:29[2]

> Let them be incorporated, that they might live.
> —ST. AUGUSTINE[3]

> The whole world is burning.
> The world fills with smoke,
> it is difficult to breathe.
> The terror and joy cannot be described!
> —NIKOLAJ VELIMIROVIĆ[4]

---

[*] This work was supported by JSPS KAKENHI Grant Number JP22KJ1922.

2. Scripture quotations in this chapter are from the RSV.

3. *In Ioannis Evangelium Tractatus* 124.26: "Accedat, credat, incorporetur, ut vivificetur"; quoted in Lubac, *Corpus Mysticum*, 1613.

4. "Song of Victory" (Победна песма), Serbian Orthodox hymn in public domain.

PART I. KENOSIS IN POLITICAL THEOLOGY

1.

THE TITLE OF THIS chapter stems from the encyclical "Mystici Corporis Christi" by Pope Pius XII, which received its name, as is custom in the Roman Catholic tradition, from the opening words of the text. The encyclical is concerned with the doctrine of the "mystical body" of Christ, "which is the church." *Doctrina mystici corporis Christi, quod est ecclesia.* First, a few preliminary remarks.

Delving into the intimidatingly vast ocean of shifting signifiers that make theological discourse, I admit speaking in fact without any theological qualification; I hold no formal authority over this subject matter. And contrary to what the title of my chapter may suggest, I will in the following not present a theological commentary on this particular encyclical, although it arguably remains one of the most important magisterial documents on ecclesiology, concerned with the nature of this very peculiar institution that is the Roman Catholic Church.

If I would have to define before you the standpoint from which I dare in a kind of childish shamelessness to speak under a title borrowed from a pope, then I do so as someone coming, in the words of a certain anthropologist, "from the other side of the moon."[5] And if I would attempt to further characterize this standpoint, I might employ the obscure term "para-theological" and metaphorically reserve myself the dubious privilege of a sideways and maybe somewhat distorted gaze.

Yet, I do wish to ask the question: How does the concept of kenosis, the "self-emptying" of Christ until death on the cross relate to the curious doctrine of the mystical body? So, let me begin by briefly recapitulating the main scriptural references for the theological *topoi* in question from the letters of St. Paul. First, again, the origin of kenosis in the Letter to the Philippians.

> Have this mind among yourselves, which is yours in Christ Jesus, who, though he was in the form of God, did not count equality with God a thing to be grasped, but emptied himself, taking the form of a servant, being born in the likeness of men. And being found in human form he humbled himself and became obedient unto death, even death on a cross. Therefore God has highly exalted him and bestowed on him the name which is above every name, that at the name of Jesus every knee should bow, in heaven and on earth and under the earth, and every tongue confess that Jesus Christ is Lord, to the glory of God the Father. (Phil 2: 5–11)

5. Lévi-Strauss, *Autre face de la lune.*

And, in his Letter to the Corinthians the exemplary use of the phrase "body of Christ" for the church collective: "Now you are the body of Christ and individually members of it" (1 Cor 12: 27; see also Col 1:18; 2:18–20; Eph 1:22–23; 3:19; 4:13).

What is ultimately at stake in linking these Pauline passages is the institutional dimension of kenosis; through becoming the "body of Christ," the institutionalization, systematization, and universalization of the kenotic love of this body as founding reference in the church kingdom. And so, although this chapter will not be an examination of the conceptual history of theology and how the syntagma "mystical body" came into use after centuries of development,[4] I will nevertheless be speaking about this peculiar *thing* (G. K. Chesterton), which is the church, who as Christ's "mystical body" (Pius XII) has, as some theologians argue, in imitation of her divine founder and "invisible head," now entered the time of her passion.

However, I will not continue before outlining a little bit further the interest that has led me to this subject matter. It is in fact through my investigation of the Japanese Kyoto School's engagement with Christianity that I found myself confronted with the necessity to inquire into theology and specifically the nature of the church institution. Nishitani Keiji, student of Kyoto School founder Nishida Kitarō, and one of the most prominent Japanese thinkers of this lineage, writes in his seminal work *Religion and Nothingness*:

> Historically . . . Christianity . . . has functioned at once as the matrix and the antagonist of modern science since its beginnings in the Renaissance or even before. It is the same with modern atheism, whose variety of forms is unthinkable apart from Christianity. If we trace the genealogy of the ideas that make up the ingredients of modern atheism—for example, the idea of a natural law of unyielding necessity, the idea of progress, and the idea of social justice that has motivated so many social revolutions—we come back eventually to Christianity.

It is this key passage and what might be called its "genealogical hypothesis" that have sent my research on its current trajectory. We are thereby confronted with the difficult questions of the genesis of "secular modernity," questions regarding the "legitimacy of the modern age" and political theology.[6]

---

6. It would be fruitful to situate the Kyoto School engagement with Christianity in the context of the debates surrounding these questions. Carl Schmitt, Jacob Taubes, Karl Löwith, Hans Blumenberg, Charles Taylor, Giorgio Agamben, Alister McGrath, and Slavoj Žižek are only some of the most important "Western" names who have shaped and contributed to these debates.

Indeed, I argue that, when seen from the standpoint of this genealogical hypothesis, the Kyoto School's engagement with the problem of "modernity" can be deciphered as a covert engagement with Christianity, the specifically Christian premises of modernity, the theological origin of specifically modern structures of political power, social order, but also of knowledge and truth, and vice versa, the engagement with Christianity as a covert struggle with modernity, as an attempt at "overcoming modernity."[7] And, most clearly in the case of Nishitani Keiji, we find that it is from Mahāyāna Buddhist sources, especially Japanese Zen, that an arsenal of signifiers is mobilized and employed in this struggle with Christianity, modernity, and the essential linkage between both.

I wish to emphasize this now all-too-often obfuscated essential antagonism at the center of religious encounter which takes place in the thought of the Kyoto School, and highlight the strategic nature of their intervention into the field of theology in their struggle with modernity. At the heart of this matter, I see an essential antagonism between the Crucified and the Awakened, between the consuming Fire and the extinguishing Void, between the principles of Selective or Elective Love and Indifferent or Objectless Compassion.[8] With these remarks, I am already jumping quite far ahead in anticipation, well beyond the scope of this chapter. However, I will have to add yet another few words to make my general intentions clearer.

What Nishitani with his genealogical hypothesis only addresses in a very broad sense as "Christianity" should be further narrowed down and specified, and I do so by laying focus on the Roman Catholic Church as the "institutional matrix" of modernity. None other than the psychoanalyst Jacques Lacan in his late years spoke, in his usual mischievous style, of the "triumph of [the true] religion," which, he adds, is the "Roman Catholic religion."[9] And this is—even if this might seem on first or maybe even second and third sight counterintuitive to the degree of absurdity—indeed, I hold, the condition under which we "moderns" find ourselves. And it is for this reason, that I would in a certain qualified sense agree with the thesis that we in fact never truly "have been modern," insofar as we nolens volens

---

7. This of course being the title of a now infamous wartime symposium in which several of those affiliated with the Kyoto School, among them most prominently Nishitani Keiji, participated. See the translation and commentary of Richard Calichman, *Overcoming Modernity*.

8. Most clearly seen by the Roman Catholic theologian Henri de Lubac in *Aspects du bouddhisme*, pt. 1.

9. Lacan, *Triomphe de la religion*.

still have this same foundation of "truth" beneath our feet, even if the boots we are wearing are now labeled "secular."

After the triumph of the *vera religio*, and the rise of the institutional matrix of the Roman Catholic Church, which constitutes itself as the "mystical body" (*corpus mysticum*) of its divine Head, Jesus Christ, we are, borrowing again from a certain vocabulary of Nishitani Keiji, now always already finding ourselves standing on a "field" (*ba* 場) of love (agape), or, more precisely, on the "distorted foundation" of kenotic love, captured within the "catholic," i.e., universal "enframing" (pace Heidegger) of what I want to term the eucharistic machinery and kenotic love economy. It is the peculiar logic of this institution of the "true religion" which has moved and shaped history in the West and beyond,[10] and it is, I argue, precisely against this institutional logic and its political theology of kenotic love that a thinker like Nishitani attempted to formulate an alternative and offer a way of escape. It is an escape offered from what already the young Nishitani in a 1928 text had called and criticized as a "distorted foundation" of the "church kingdom and its colossal theological architecture."[11] An escape from what I am tempted to call the essentially Roman Catholic "empire of love."

This is the rather obscure and immodest proposal of a grand narrative, of which I here can only present some fragments gathered in a nutshell under my equally immodest papal chapter title. A grand narrative, drawing a historical line from the kenosis of Christ to the kenosis of the institution which, while following a very precise logic of imitation, claims to be his "mystical body." This narrative will ultimately, I hope, provide an adequate background for reexamining the confrontation between Buddhism and Christianity, found in an exemplary way in the works of the Kyoto School and Kyoto School philosopher Nishitani Keiji.

2.

In his study titled *The Disenchantment of the World*, historian and sociologist Marcel Gauchet has produced something akin to a Foucauldian analysis of the "dispositif" of the Roman Catholic Church, the structural logic of this institution and the historical ramifications of its rise to power. I quote a crucial passage at length:

10. As, among many others, historian of law Pierre Legendre has convincingly argued throughout his works. I will comment on Legendre in more detail below.
11. Nishitani, *Collected Works*, 165.

> At the origins of the Church's existence was a special type of mediating claim, one grafted directly onto the Christ-centered mediation it tried to make permanent. Christ revealed the abyss between the human and the divine by showing that God's will could only reach us through the Word becoming flesh. By this fact, by the immeasurable gap between the human words through which we have received this will and the infinite wisdom behind them, this abyss became something we had to continually contemplate and interpret. In other words, the purpose of the Incarnation was to open up a yawning gap hermeneutically impossible to close. And it was the Church's nature to be at the heart of the irreparable gap between the message and its source, in order to both embody its conspicuous obviousness and fill it. The Church's position, ambition and role made it a wholly original institution: the first bureaucracy to give history meaning, the first administration of ultimate meaning. It had to administer a definitively determined doctrine and body of regulations. On the one hand, it had to constantly redefine them, dispel the shadows, remove uncertainties, and determine their dogmatic content; on the other, it had to examine all their possible ramifications, so as to maintain a living communication between the spirit and the letter. The Church's claim to authority arises from a central openness onto the abyss of truth, to which it continually calls attention, while striving to mitigate the vertigo that abyss induced.[12]

Certainly, as Gauchet observes here, it is the logic of the incarnation which is foundational to the logic of the church institution as she defines herself as mystical corporation precisely through imitation of the Word's incarnation. And, just as Gauchet argues, this logic of incarnation indeed introduces what may be called a kind of "hyper-transcendence" into history, which tears open a gap and marks the momentary opening of an abyss of indistinguishability between transcendence and immanence, identity and difference, eternity and time, life and death (borrowing a celebrated term from Nicolaus Cusanus, we might speak of the "non-aliud" of incarnation).

Furthermore, although Gauchet himself does not explicitly touch upon this concept, the move towards the abyss of indistinguishable hyper-transcendence can easily be identified as the kenotic process. Paradoxically, it is through the increased proximity between creator and creature in the Word's kenotic assumption of our mortal flesh that hermeneutically an even greater distance is introduced between both. There can be no doubt that the

---

12. Gauchet, *Disenchantment of the World*, 135.

hermeneutic system and dogmatic constitution of the church magisterium is built around this abyss and has produced so many attempts to suture this central gap with meaning.

And yet, what Gauchet fails to adequately address in his study, is that the church as "bureaucracy" and "administration of ultimate meaning" does not consist merely of a developing plurality of interpretations circling around the hermeneutic abyss of the "fact" of incarnation. For there is what I want to call a singular "sovereign interpretation" at the foundation of this hermeneutic system. And it is precisely through this sovereign interpretation that the hermeneutic gap introduced through the kenotic assumption of flesh can be "closed." This interpretation in its peculiar formal structure as well as in its concrete content as supreme referent, defines and determines in the last instance all derivative meaning flowing through the doctrinal apparatus of the church institution.

What I call the sovereign interpretation refers to the eucharistic interpretation given by Christ himself to his own anticipated death during the Last Supper in the "upper room" on Maundy Thursday, in anticipation of his crucifixion on Good Friday. It is in this anticipatory eucharistic interpretation of the murder of God, an anticipation which in a peculiar temporal structure will only be realized in its full meaning retrospectively through its repetition, after the risen Christ's appearance in Emmaus (Luke 24: 30–35), that the church institution fully finds its supreme referent; freely making use of the celebrated terms of Martin Heidegger, one might also speak of a "formal indication" of Christ's divine "being-towards-death," which fulfils itself only in the sacrificial act of the cross. And the historical significance and ramifications of this sovereign interpretation for the constitution of the church structure cannot be overstated.

It is arguably this initial anticipation and interpretation of the meaning of "God's death" at the heart of the gospel, on which the institutional operations and whole sacramental function of the church are founded. The mystery of the Eucharist can be deciphered as a concrete interpretation of kenosis; turning the murder of God into his anticipated voluntary act of self-sacrifice, manifesting, in the words of St. Maximus the Confessor, a divine "death wish."[13] And it is this divine death wish that drives the institution and salvific economy of the church. For precisely this reason, it seems to me to be ultimately mistaken to reduce, as Gauchet seems to suggest, the Roman Catholic institution to a hermeneutic system of symbolic meaning

---

13. "Christ's divine will wished for death"; quoted in Balthasar, *Cosmic Liturgy*, 265.

production. Within the framework of the Roman Catholic institution, the sovereign interpretation of the Word's kenotic assumption of flesh cannot be reduced to a signifying operation, but must be seen in its sacrificial nature; we are therefore confronted not just with signifiers among signifiers, but *sacra signa*: sacraments.

In the eucharistic scene, constituting the founding reference of all theologically meaningful interpretations, meaning is not produced, but ultimately consumed in the act of communion. The exceptional gap torn into the ontological fabric of the world through the incarnation of the Word is indeed "hermeneutically" impossible to close, i.e., no produced meaning can fill this gap. Instead, following the sovereign interpretation, the Word become flesh situated in that very gap must be actually consumed.

However, in the act of communion, we are in fact confronted with a scene of mutual consumption.[14] When communion is received, the faithful partake in the sacrifice of the true "paschal lamb"; they devour the flesh and blood of their savior, the incarnate Word, but in this "eucharistic consumption" they do per definition not, as with ordinary food, assimilate its substance to their body and its fallen mortal flesh. On the contrary, they mysteriously "become what they eat" and are consumed by Christ. "When they eat, they are eaten, and when they are eaten, they eat."[15]

"From the Kenotic Christ to the Kenotic Church" is how I subtitled my chapter; and what I now wish to highlight with these rudimentary reflections sketched out above, is how the transition from the singular Christ in history to the church as *totus Christus* (St. Augustine) and "mystical body" hinges on the institutional function of the Eucharist as sovereign interpretation of kenosis. It is in the eucharistic mystery, before all secondary theological interpretation, that kenosis finds its concrete institutional form, sacramental efficacy and reality in history.

When examining the peculiar logic of this eucharistic scene, we encounter a triadic structure that seems to me quite typical for the Roman Catholic institutional design. Here, we can speak of the triadic structure between (1) the singular paradigmatic case of Christ as is told to have appeared in history, (2) the particular individual followers of Christ, and (3) the totality of their collective body as church, formed and mediated through

14. Theologically, the twofold movement involved here could be further articulated through the vertical axis of offering the sacrifice of the Son to the Father and the horizontal axis of the distribution of grace among creation and especially the faithful through participating in this offering.

15. St. Bernard; quoted in Lubac, *Corpus Mysticum*, 15.

each individual's relation to the singular and paradigmatic exception that is Christ himself. The relation between the particulars and their totality is mediated through an exemplary exception. And it is through the unfolding of this triadic structure that the mystical body is constituted.

Translated into a terminology which emphasizes the dynamic relations between these elements of the triad, we could speak of the relation between the three moments of incarnation, imitation, and incorporation. In Christ, the Word has become incarnate. The particular baptized Christians imitate Christ, ideally and most perfectly through their participation in his sacrifice at the altar of the cross, in the eucharistic mystery. Through this Christ-imitating participation they continue to be incorporated and unified within the totality of the collective body of the church as *totus Christus*.

Finally, returning to the analysis of Marcel Gauchet, the church can indeed be described as an "administration of ultimate meaning." However, in regard to the Roman Catholic institution it is entirely insufficient to reduce this "ultimate meaning" to a hermeneutical production through magisterial interpretation of only symbolic value. Insofar as the church as "mystical body" is anchored in the Eucharist through the sovereign interpretation of the kenotic act of self-sacrifice, i.e., anchored in the divine "death wish" realized in eucharistic communion, that which is "administered" does not exhaust itself in symbolic "meaning," but has to be inscribed into the register of the Real.

3.

I will now escalate the thesis which I am advancing a little bit further. Although Marcel Gauchet is certainly one of the authors who analyze in great and convincing detail how the institutional structure of the Roman Catholic Church and the spread of Christianity through the vehicle of this structure has been of inestimable importance for the history of the "West" and beyond, I have so far only highlighted certain aspects internal to the theological self-understanding of the church.

As I already briefly mentioned in the preliminary remarks of this chapter, the thesis I am advancing goes well beyond just a reexamination of Roman Catholic ecclesiology. The "genealogical hypothesis" I found at work in the thought of Nishitani Keiji proposes a reading of history that sees the problems of "modernity" as referring back to a genealogical origin in Christianity and Christian theology. My exploration of the Roman

Catholic ecclesiology is an attempt at understanding this genealogical hypothesis. In what sense then can the Roman Catholic ecclesiology, Christ as the "mystical body," formed through participation in the self-sacrificial act of eucharistic kenosis, be addressed as the institutional matrix even of the modern, so-called "secular age"? Certainly, any sufficient answer is well outside the possible scope of this chapter. I will however add some more fragments that might contribute to such an answer.

As the historian of law Pierre Legendre has persistently pointed out throughout his works, Christianity, unlike the other "religions of the book," constitutes a historical anomaly, in that it does not prescribe any rules for social order. Instead, we find the "fulfillment of all law" in the imperative of love. And this love is first and foremost the kenotic love celebrated in its eucharistic form. Put differently, at its core, the Christian institutional order is not founded on any mythical principle which can be determined through supreme attributes, true, good, or beautiful, but precisely on the voluntary self-sacrifice and self-emptying of any such mythical foundation and on voluntary (albeit temporary) renunciation of all such attributes in the name of love, furthermore on the "communication" of this love through universal participation in the eucharistic mystery in imitation of the kenotic Christ.

For this reason, Legendre will also speak of a certain "Schize" characterizing the institutional design of Christian social order, inaugurated through the paradigmatic rise of the Roman Catholic Church.[16] Specifically, through what Legendre already in his doctoral dissertation identified as "the penetration of Roman law into classical canon law,"[17] approaching a decisive climax with what Eugen Rosenstock-Huessy and his student Harold Berman have termed the "Papal Revolution," beginning in the eleventh century under Pope Gregory VII.[18] This is not the place to elaborate on this in detail. I only wish to state what seems to me most crucial about this complex development.

Aptly summarized under Gregory VII's plan of a *reformatio totius orbis*,[19] the specifically Christian source of authority, its founding principle and supreme referent, the name of love, through a historically unprecedented will to power, systematically instrumentalizes the remnants of Roman imperial law as a convenient technology for the further construction

---

16. Legendre, *Autre Bible de l'Occident*, 487.
17. Legendre, *Pénétration du droit romain*.
18. Rosenstock-Huessy, *Out of Revolution*; Berman, *Law and Revolution*.
19. Legendre, "Reformatio totius orbis."

of the Roman Catholic institutional order. And the following centuries, from Renaissance to Reformation to Revolution, will have been nothing but a series of attempts to rebel against this papal presumption of universal and absolute power under the name of love, or to deny in one way or another the monopoly of love under papal "dictatorship" inside the Roman Catholic order. It is not least for this very reason that Marcel Gauchet could define Christianity as the "religion of heresy" and even as the "religion of man's exit from religion."[20]

Nevertheless, the will to power of the church institution ultimately did serve the purpose to propagate the gospel of kenotic love. And through the centuries of struggle against pagan mythologies, superstition, idolatry, false philosophies, heresies, all the powers and principalities of this world in the name of love, kenotic love as the "hegemonic referent," the ultimate founding principle and master signifier, the final "name of the Father," will prove successful in breaking all hegemonies and reducing all other principles of political legitimacy to nought; inducing through its spread in history a total "kenosis of grounds" (borrowing an expression from the Heideggerian philosopher Reiner Schürmann) in the name of love.[21]

The church institution thus has become paradigmatic precisely in spreading its constitutional "Schize" through the propaganda of kenotic love of the cross as the only "true" master signifier; devaluing and emptying out all mythical foundations of law and social order, and at the same time reducing all legal constructions to mere convenient instruments of power, essentially severed from the source of their authority, value, and meaning. No one has captured this radically subversive effect of the "love of the cross" in its historical reality better than the Lutheran philosopher G. W. F. Hegel. In his *Lectures on the Philosophy of Religion* we read:

> In connection with this death [of Christ on the cross] we have to notice first of all what is one of its special characteristics, namely, its polemical attitude towards outward things. Not only is the act whereby the natural will yields itself up here represented in a sensible form, but all that is peculiar to the individual, all those interests and personal ends with which the natural will can occupy itself, all that is great and counted as of value in the world, is at the same time buried in the grave of the Spirit. This is the revolutionary element by means of which the world is given a totally new form.... The cross is transfigured, what according to the

20. Gauchet, *Disenchantment of the World*, 80.
21. Schürmann, *Broken Hegemonies*.

> common idea is lowest, what the state characterises as degrading, is transformed into what is highest. Death is natural, every man must die. But since degradation is made the highest honour, all those ties that bind human society together are attacked in their foundations, are shaken and dissolved. When the cross has been elevated to the place of a banner, and is made a banner in fact, the positive content of which is at the same time the Kingdom of God, inner feeling is in the very heart of its nature detached from civil and state life, and the substantial basis of this latter is taken away, so that the whole structure has no longer any reality, but is an empty appearance, which must soon come crashing down, and make manifest in actual existence that it is no longer anything having inherent existence.[22]

It is precisely through the logic of this development that Gregory VII's plan of a *reformatio totius orbis* was in fact realized, paradoxically facilitated *through* and at the same time *against* the Roman Catholic Church. The above description of Hegel can furthermore be fruitfully juxtaposed with the words of a public address of Pope Benedict XVI, whom I also quote at length:

> Christ is always reborn in every generation and thus he assumes the gathering of humanity within Himself. And this cosmic birth is achieved in the cry of the Cross, in the suffering of the Passion. And the blood of the martyrs belongs to this cry of the Cross. So, at this moment, we can look at . . . Psalm 81, where we can see part of this process. God is among gods; they are still considered as gods in Israel. In this Psalm, in a great concentration, in a prophetic vision, we can see the power taken from the gods. Those that seemed gods are not gods, lose their divine characteristics, and fall to earth. *Dii estis et moriemini sicut homines* (cf. Ps 81: 6–7): the weakening of power, the fall of the divinities. This process that is achieved along the path of faith of Israel, and which is summed up here in one vision, is the true process of the history of religion: the fall of the gods. And thus the transformation of the world, the knowledge of the true God, the loss of power by the forces that dominate the world, is a process of suffering. In the history of Israel we can see how this liberation from polytheism, this recognition.
>
> "Only He is God" is achieved with great pain, beginning with the path of Abraham, the exile, the Maccabeans, to Christ. And this process of the loss of power, spoken in the Book of Revelation,

---

22. Hegel, *Lectures on Philosophy of Religion*, 3:89.

chapter 12 continues throughout history; it mentions the fall of the angels, which are not truly angels, they are not divinities on earth. And it is achieved truly, right at the time of the rising Church, where we can see how with the blood of the martyrs comes the weakening of the divinities, starting with the divine emperor, from all these divinities. It is the blood of the martyrs, the suffering, the cry of Mother Church that brings about their fall and thus transforms the world. This fall is not only the knowledge that they are not God; it is the process of transformation of the world, which costs blood, costs the suffering of witnesses of Christ. And, if we look closely, we can see that this process never ends. It is achieved in various periods of history in ever new ways; even today, at this moment in which Christ, the only Son of God, must be born for the world with the fall of the gods, with pain, the martyrdom of witnesses.[23]

Now, through this "true process of the history of religion," precisely insofar as the church institution can understand herself and her role in this process as the mystical body in imitation of and in unity with Christ, the dissolution of the Roman Catholic institution can paradoxically be interpreted as her martyrdom, offering herself in imitation of the kenotic Christ in a total Eucharist corresponding to the *totus Christus*. Such a total Eucharist would certainly be part of the reason why, with Jacques Lacan, we can speak of a "triumph of the true religion," even at a point in history when radical defeat seems so much more plausible.

Within the long trajectory leading from the kenotic Christ to the kenotic church, we could then draw a more concrete line of historical development from Pope Gregory VII to Paul VI, who, like no other pope before him, has become a symbol for the voluntary kenotic self-dissolution or "auto-deconstruction" of the modern church.[24] Indeed, this roughly thousand-year trajectory, from the church at the height of its glory and power in the eleventh century to a voluntary self-renunciation to the point of an ecclesial "lunar eclipse" and unprecedented inner turmoil in the twentieth century, has led to an act of eucharistic consumption of the mystical body, which, under the name of secularization, marks a total reversal from the *imitatio imperii* (see Ernst Percy Schramm) of the church to an *imitatio sacerdoti* of the worldly powers now known as the state, and thus, under a

23. Benedict XVI, "Special Assembly for Middle East."
24. Nancy, *Déconstruction du christianisme*.

new form of pastoral governance (see Michel Foucault) the dissemination and paradoxical triumph of kenotic love.

4.

I will now come to the end of this chapter with some concluding remarks. In a recent interview, mourning the seemingly desolate situation of the "modernized" Catholic Church after the Second Vatican Council, the superior general of the highly controversial and ultraconservative Priestly Society of St. Pius X, Fr. Davide Pagliarani, said the following remarkable words:

> Here we wonder whether we are in the presence of a heresy or, quite simply, of a "nothingness" that we cannot even describe. A heretic, in fact, still "believes" in something, and may still have an idea of the Church, even if his idea is distorted. However, here we are dealing with an idea of the Church that is not only fuzzy but also "liquid," to use a modern expression. Here they advocate a Church without doctrine, without dogma, without faith, and in which there is no longer any need for an authority to teach anything. Everything is dissolved into a spirit of "love and service," without really knowing what this means—if it means anything at all—and to where it leads.[25]

Remarkable words indeed, for it would be certainly quite difficult to say how the "dissolution into a spirit of 'love and service'" would be in and of itself lamentable, and for a Christian no less! And even if the loss of "knowledge" to the point of total dementia does seem to give some reason for legitimate concern, did not the great bishop of Hippo himself teach that knowledge is no more than a useful machine (*tamquam machina quaedam*), a scaffolding that will be destroyed when love has triumphed, once and for all?[26]

I would therefore like to end my chapter with some words of reassurance for the concerned superior general. Not only did kenotic love so far essentially triumph above all other principles of legitimacy, so that the anarchy of love is well on its way to assume the status of humanity's final "hegemonic fantasm" (Reiner Schürmann), humanity's final dream with

---

25. FSSPX.Actualités, "Interview," para. 17.

26. Augustine, epis. 55, 21, 39, esp.: "Sic itaque adhibeatur scientia tanquam machina quaedam, per quam structura caritatis assurgat quae maneat in aeternum, etiam cum scientia destruetur" (further bibliographic information unavailable).

the cross as its "navel" (Freud), and thus to become the last name of power and legitimate political agency.[27] We can also already see new hierarchies forming, modeled more or less explicitly after the supreme sacramental efficiency of the Roman Catholic Church.[28] Hierarchies in an "empire of management"[29] that will "take care"[30] of all political, economic, social, and personal grievances, through the management and distribution, like the hierarchy they are modeled after, of the only resource that matters: love.

BIBLIOGRAPHY

Agamben, Giorgio. *Opus Dei: An Archaeology of Duty*. Translated by Adam Kotsko. Meridian: Crossing Aesthetics. Stanford, CA: Stanford University Press, 2013.

Balthasar, Hans Urs von. *Cosmic Liturgy: The Universe According to Maximus the Confessor*. Communio. San Francisco: Ignatius, 2003.

Benedict XVI. "Special Assembly for the Middle East of the Synod of Bishops: Meditation of His Holiness Benedict XVI During the First General Congregation." Vatican, Oct. 11, 2010. https://www.vatican.va/content/benedict-xvi/en/speeches/2010/october/documents/hf_ben-xvi_spe_20101011_meditazione.html.

Berman, Harold J. *Law and Revolution*. 2 vols. Cambridge, MA: Belknap, 2006.

Calichman, Richard F., ed. and trans. *Overcoming Modernity: Cultural Identity in Wartime Japan*. Weatherhead Books on Asia. New York: Columbia University Press, 2008.

FSSPX.Actualités. "Interview with the Superior General of the Priestly Society of Saint Pius X." SSPX, May 5, 2023. https://fsspx.org/en/publications/interview-superior-general-priestly-society-saint-pius-x-36243.

Gauchet, Marcel. *The Disenchantment of the World: A Political History of Religion*. Translated by Oscar Burge. Princeton, NJ: Princeton University Press, 1999.

Girard, René. *Je vois Satan tomber comme l'éclair*. Biblio essais. Paris: Livre de Poche, 2001.

Groys, Boris. *Philosophy of Care*. London: Verso, 2022.

Hegel, G. W. F. *Lectures on the Philosophy of Religion*. Translated by E. B. Speirs and J. Burdon Sanderson. 3 vols. London: Paul, Trench, Trübner, 1895.

Lacan, Jacques. "*Le triomphe de la religion*": *Précédé de "Discours aux catholiques."* Paris: Seuil, 2005.

Legendre, Pierre. *L'autre Bible de l'Occident: Le monument romano-canonique; Études sur l'architecture dogmatique des sociétés*. Leçons 9. Paris: Fayard, 2009.

———. *Dominium mundi: L'empire du management*. 1001 Nights. Paris: Fayard, 2007.

———. *La pénétration du droit romain dans le droit canonique classique de Gratien à Innocent IV (1140–1254)*. Paris: Jouve, 1964.

———. "Reformatio totius orbis. Überlegungen zum Universalismus des abendländischen Christentums. Erzählung aus melancholischen Zeiten." In

---

27. Girard, *Je vois Satan tomber*.
28. Agamben, *Opus Dei*.
29. Legendre, *Dominium mundi*.
30. Groys, *Philosophy of Care*.

Paulus-Lektüren, 221–40. Paderborn, Germ.: Wilhelm Fink, 2013. https://doi.org/10.30965/9783846753125_012.

Lévi-Strauss, Claude. *L'autre face de la lune: Écrits sur le Japon*. Sciences humaines: La librairie du XXIe siècle. Paris: Seuil, 2005.

Lubac, Henri de. *Aspects du bouddhisme*. Vol. 21 of *Oeuvres complète*. Paris: Cerf, 2005.

———. *Corpus Mysticum: The Eucharist and the Church in the Middle Ages*. Edited by Laurence Paul Hemming and Susan Frank Parsons. Translated by Gemma Simmonds with Richard Price. Faith in Reason. London: SCM, 2011.

Nancy, Jean-Luc. *Déconstruction du christianisme*. 2 vols. La philosophie en effet. Paris: Galilée, 2005, 2010.

Nishitani, Keiji. 西谷啓治著作集第二巻 [*Tyosakushu*, Collected works]. Vol. 2. Tokyo: Sōbunsha, 1987.

———. *Religion and Nothingness*. Translated by Jan van Bragt. Nanzan Studies in Religion and Culture. Berkeley: University of California Press, 1982.

Pius XII. "*Mystici Corporis Christi*: On the Mystical Body of Christ." Vatican, June 29, 1943. https://www.vatican.va/content/pius-xii/en/encyclicals/documents/hf_p-xii_enc_29061943_mystici-corporis-christi.html.

Rosenstock-Huessy, Eugen. *Out of Revolution: Autobiography of Western Man*. Providence, RI: Berg, 1993.

Schürmann, Reiner. *Broken Hegemonies*. Bloomington: Indiana University Press, 2003.

4

Kenosis in Contemporary Continental Philosophy[1]

From Deconstruction to Phenomenology

NIKOLAAS CASSIDY-DEKETELAERE

INTRODUCTION

IN RECENT YEARS, THE Pauline term of "kenosis" has become a central motif in certain corners of Continental philosophy, particularly among authors who are nevertheless not engaged in overt theologizing, but for whom it becomes a metaphor for deconstruction (including but not limited to Jean-Luc Nancy, Catherine Malabou, and Jacques Derrida).[2] This development has, however, gone largely unnoticed and its significance therefore remains insufficiently appreciated. Diagnosing what I propose to call the "kenotic turn" of Continental philosophy, I will argue that Paul's kenosis has been philosophically appropriated so as to indicate the point within the Christian theological complex that constitutes its fatal agent by setting in motion its own self-deconstruction or de-theologization. This

---

1. This chapter is a revised and abridged version of the introduction to my book *Jean-Luc Nancy*.

2. Though I will stick to simply observing this common interest, a more detailed account is offered by Baird, "Whose *Kenosis*?"

dynamic, which implies that every engagement with theology ultimately carries itself outside of theology proper, will then allow us reconceive the predominant style of Continental philosophy of religion, namely phenomenology's so-called "theological turn": in their right *turn towards* theology, the philosopher must be careful not to simply remain stuck there, for it serves their investigation only insofar as this engagement is precisely what allows them to *turn away* from "the theological," or for phenomenology de-theologize itself. In other words, by drawing out the kenotic motif in contemporary Continental philosophy and connecting it to phenomenology's theological turn, I will argue that what is needed now is a *deconstruction of the theological turn*. This, I suggest, can be accomplished by way of what I would call—if only in a programmatic way—a "phenomenology of kenosis," namely: a phenomenology that *starts from* theology (Paul's notion of kenosis), precisely so as to *move beyond* it (to de-theologize itself). However, this phenomenology will not actually be developed here, since my aim in this chapter is simply to outline the "kenotic turn" and illustrate its broader significance for the field, namely how it allows us to reconceive or to "think after" the so-called "theological turn." Nevertheless, the present investigation, perhaps like the theological turn itself, certainly constitutes a first (theological) step *towards* such a phenomenology of kenosis, even if the (philosophical and phenomenological) destination is thereby not yet reached.

To make this step, I will first give an overview of the present state of Continental philosophy of religion, noting in particular that the "return of religion"—which arguably defines the scope of the field—is actually composed of two distinct movements: the "theological turn" is only one of these, since there is a parallel set of authors who all approach religion through the lens of Paul's kenosis. Subsequently, I will discuss a few examples from this second set of authors. Finally, I conclude with a programmatic section that, though it must still remain somewhat abstract and provisional, proposes what "thinking after the theological turn" by way of a "phenomenology of kenosis" might mean and how it is significant to the field of Continental philosophy (of religion).

THE AMBIGUOUS RETURN OF RELIGION

With philosophers collectively turning to religious themes and language, the "return of religion" is a widely *observed* fact that has nevertheless been *described* rather inadequately. This is partly due to "religion" inevitably proving impossible to define, though we may pragmatically understand this "return" here as the use philosophers make of theological texts and language. However, more importantly, scholarship has generally insufficiently recognized that this "return" is made up of two distinct "turns" to religion, or two different ways of making philosophical use of theology. If religion then returns to philosophy, it does so in a highly ambiguous way.

First, there is the movement known as the *theological turn*, comprising a set of prominent French religious thinkers of the 1980s and 1990s (Emmanuel Levinas, Jean-Luc Marion, Michel Henry, and Jean-Louis Chrétien) who placed those specific experiences that can be considered "religious" at the center of the phenomenological investigation into the general structure of experience.[3] This immediately drew accusations of an unwarranted theologization of philosophy that have not died down since, notably by Dominique Janicaud's *The Theological Turn of French Phenomenology*.[4] Meanwhile, in parallel though ostensibly unconnected, a broader set of apparently atheist thinkers (e.g., Jürgen Habermas, Alain Badiou, Jean-Luc Nancy, Slavoj Žižek, etc.) began unearthing the roots of Western modernity in the theological structure of the Christian religion—this development has become known as the *post-secular turn*.[5] These two movements, which together comprise philosophy's "return to religion," nevertheless "turn" to "religion" in very different ways: whilst the theological turn grounds philosophical reflection in a theological dimension, the post-secular turn uncovers to what extent modern thought remains innervated by theology in an attempt to articulate a more authentic atheism.[6] In short, one is theological, the other (aspires to be) post-theological: the first *returns* to religion in order to *turn towards* the theological dimension, the second does so only in an attempt to *turn away* from it.

Existing scholarship has neglected this split in the "return of religion," often focussing exclusively on the post-secular turn insofar as its insight are useful to cultural theory. For example, in *Return Statements: The Return of Religion in Contemporary Philosophy*, Gregg Lambert speaks casually of the

---

3. See Courtine, *Phénoménologie et théologie*.
4. See Janicaud, "Theological Turn."
5. For examples, see Habermas, *Between Naturalism and Religion*; Badiou, *Saint Paul*; Žižek, *Puppet and Dwarf*. For an overview, see McLennan, "Postsecular Turn"; Latré et al., *Radical Secularisation?*; De Vries and Sullivan, *Political Theologies*.
6. Of course, this leaves undecided whether they are successful in articulating a more authentic atheism. See Watkin, *Difficult Atheism*.

"theological and/or post-secular turn"[7] and focusses—despite the title of his book—on "the 'post-secular turn' . . ., even though there is a tradition that dates to a much earlier period in French phenomenological circles, namely from the early 1980s."[8] Hent de Vries, in *Philosophy and the Turn to Religion*, likewise distances his inquiry from Marion or (parts of) Levinas, since they "opt for a purely theological . . . discourse."[9] Instead, he is interested in authors like Heidegger or Derrida, whose "turn to religion . . . does not signal a return to theology or religion per se," since "religion is never conceived of as the hidden meaning of a secular historical or anthropological truth," and instead "show that citations from religious traditions are more fundamental to the structure of language and experience than the genealogies, critiques, and transcendental reflections of the modern discourse that has deemed such citations obsolete."[10] Yet, in the theological turn, theology and religion are very much returned to: religious or theophanic experience becomes the touchstone for the phenomenological analysis of experience more generally, and Marion in particular identifies this experience with the revelation of Christ.

The scholarship of philosophy's return to religion has thus been confused on two levels. Firstly, it neglects the difference between authors who (re)turn to theology and those who try to think beyond it.[11] John Caputo is one of the few scholars escaping this charge, recognizing the difference as one between phenomenological (e.g., Marion and Henry) and deconstructive (e.g., Derrida and Nancy) approaches in recent philosophy of religion: "If deconstruction has taken a 'religious' turn, this is a religion without theology, representing . . . a religious but 'a-theological' turn . . . , while the new phenomenology has taken a decidedly 'theological turn.'"[12] In short, they (re)turn to religion in different ways: "It comes down to the difference between a *theological* and an *atheological* religion," and thus two distinct (re)turns, "the one with and the other without attachment to a determinate

---

7. Lambert, *Return Statements*, 6.
8. Lambert, *Return Statements*, 1.
9. De Vries, *Philosophy*, 26.
10. De Vries, *Philosophy*, 2.
11. Other works that fail to make this distinction include Blond, *Post-Secular Philosophy*; A. Smith and Whistler, *After the Postsecular*. A possible exception, insofar as it at least recognizes the distinction, is Staudigl and Alvis, *Phenomenology*.
12. Caputo, "Hyperbolization of Phenomenology," 69.

theological tradition."[13] Implicit in Caputo's formulation also lies the second confusion of the existing scholarship, namely that the atheological turn to religion would be but an exposition of the "post-secular" condition: a philosophy of culture, rather than a philosophical style as such.

Yet, these projects nevertheless extend far beyond Christianity, modern society or even metaphysical reason.[14] Here, I therefore suggest reconceiving the "post-secular" turn by way of a theological figure many of its authors draw on: namely, what Paul describes as the kenosis of Christ, or God's self-emptying (*ekenosen*) of divinity by assuming the human condition in the incarnation (Phil 2:7). This dynamic, characteristic of the Christian God, becomes characteristic of Christianity as such in the authors of the "post-secular" turn: Christianity is the religion that empties itself out of its religious or theological character into secular modernity. In Marcel Gauchet's famous phrase, Christianity is "the religion of the egress [*sortie*] from religion."[15] Yet, as the implications of this philosophical gesture exceed the question of the relationship between Christianity and modern society, I would suggest that philosophy's return to religion is comprised by the *theological turn*, on the one hand, and the *kenotic turn*, on the other.

The authors of the kenotic turn, unlike their colleagues comprising the theological turn, are not interested in theological notions like kenosis for Christianity's sake, as a theologian would be; they explore them only to the extent that the "death of God" (Nietzsche), the "de-theologization" (Heidegger), or "de-Christianization" (Derrida) characteristic of modern thought is itself a product of Christian theology's self-effacing (i.e., kenotic) structure: the *turn towards* Christian "theology" (its language and texts), paradoxically serves the distinctly philosophical purpose of *turning away* from "the theological" (Derrida's metaphysics of presence or Heidegger's onto-theology). Nancy's "deconstruction of Christianity," for example, describes how, as theological-metaphysical construct, Christianity equally de-theologizes or deconstructs itself as Christianity: due to its characteristic kenotic doctrine of God (divinity's self-effacement), it sets in motion its own de-theologization or secularization (Christianity's self-effacement). The divine self-emptying denoted by the theological notion of kenosis thus

13. Caputo, "Hyperbolization of Phenomenology," 89–90.

14. For examples of this reading, see Hutchens, *Jean-Luc Nancy*, 85–102; Alexandrova et al., *Re-Treating Religion*.

15. Gauchet, *Disenchantment of the World* (translation modified); quoted in Nancy, *Dis-Enclosure*, 142.

serves only as the means for elaborating the implications of the death of God, for thinking "atheologically." These authors therefore do not primarily understand kenosis theologically, but articulate what it might mean once pushed—precisely *according to its proper logic*—towards its own de-theologization. In other words, kenosis as a piece of Christian theology is what provides the egress (*sortie*) not just *from* theology but precisely *as* theology: it is only by *turning towards* theology (i.e., starting from the theological notion of kenosis) that phenomenology will be able to *turn away* from theology (i.e., to "de-theologize" itself or move beyond theology)—which is what I understand here by thinking *after the theological turn*.

KENOSIS IN PHILOSOPHY

The philosophical appropriation of the kenotic motif goes back to Hegel, who gives kenosis its philosophical reach by understanding the whole of reality—not just Christ's humanity—in terms of Luther's German translation of the Greek word (*Entäußerung*), namely as the externalization of Absolute Spirit.[16] This exercise then extends all the way up to Derrida, who latches onto negative theology as operating a "kenosis of discourse," like the one performed above (e.g., power in weakness).[17] This has resulted in several recent studies applying the kenotic motif to a range of philosophical problems (e.g., subjectivity, experience, language).[18] I will therefore now give a brief overview of the most significant recent philosophical appropriations of the kenotic motif.

Levinas's Jewish Kenosis

Emmanuel Levinas is difficult to categorise in my theological-atheological (or kenotic) schematization of contemporary philosophy: though his phenomenology of the infinite undeniably makes it possible, Levinas himself refrains from Marion's (revelation) and Henry's (incarnation)

---

16. Hegel, *Phenomenology of Spirit*, 457. For commentary, see Dawe, *Form of a Servant*, 104–26; Dubilet, *Self-Emptying Subject*, 92–122.

17. Derrida, *On the Name*, 71. For commentary, see De Vries, *Philosophy*, 305–58; Caputo, *Prayers and Tears of Jacques Derrida*, 1–68.

18. For examples, see Dubilet, *Self-Emptying Subject*; Van Riessen, *Man as Place of God*; Zijlstra, *Letting Go*.

overt theologizing.[19] Obviously, Levinas is not a Christian, and is therefore far less eager to model experience generally on the Christian theological model. When it comes to the appropriation of the concepts of Christian theology, such as kenosis, Levinas therefore finds himself in the same position as the authors of the "kenotic turn": namely, drawing on the language of a tradition he remains outside of in order to think broader philosophical problems.

When invited to speak about the incarnation, Levinas admits as much: "I do not have the effrontery to enter an area forbidden to those who do not share the faith, and the ultimate dimensions of which no doubt escape me," instead he merely wants "to reflect" on "the multiple meanings suggested by the notion of Man-God." This includes kenosis as "the idea of a self-inflicted humiliation on the part of the Supreme Being, of a descent of the Creator to the level of the Creature."[20] Of course, Levinas does not believe that God humbled himself in Christ, his interest in this notion is therefore not that of the theologian. Instead, he wants to explore "to what extent these ideas, which have unconditional value for the Christian faith, have philosophical value, and to what extent they can appear in phenomenology." This is also the approach taken by the authors of the kenotic turn: namely, investigating what Christian theological notions mean outside of or beyond their immediate context. Their philosophical and theological meanings cannot straightforwardly be identified. Levinas therefore cautions: "I ask myself to what extent the new categories we have just described are philosophical. I am certain that this extent will be judged insufficient by the believing Christian."[21] This apparent insufficiency for the theologian of the philosophical treatment of Christian concepts is not due to the limitations of philosophy's perspective compared to theology's, but to a divergence in the respective concerns orienting them. This distinction is what, for example, the Anglican theologian Graham Ward fails to recognize when, himself tracking the philosophical appropriation of the kenotic motif since Hegel, he complains that "what is absent from modernity's concept of kenosis is the role played by theological discourse as response to a reception of and

---

19. As illustrated, for example, by Levinas's highly cautious approach when he does address God directly, but precisely only insofar as God gives himself to thought (*vient à l'idée*), in *Of God Who Comes to Mind*.

20. Levinas, *Entre Nous*, 53.

21. Levinas, *Entre Nous*, 54.

participation in the divine."[22] Yet, to philosophically appropriate the concept of kenosis means precisely to expropriate it from theological discourse: it is articulated by people who do not recognize the divinity it is supposedly participating in. Ward's complaint presupposes that the Christian theological viewpoint has both priority and ultimate authority, ruling out from the start that an outside or philosophical perspective on its concepts might be useful to that theology (in phenomenology's appropriation), or that its concepts speak beyond their immediate religious context (in Christianity's self-deconstruction). Levinas's goal is not to satisfy the theologian, but to interest the philosopher.

What Levinas finds philosophically interesting about kenosis is that, as "the humiliation of God," it "allows for conceiving the relationship with transcendence in terms other than those of naiveté." Christianity's innovation is that, compared to the pagan religions where the gods likewise manifest themselves among men, the Christian God manifests its divinity precisely in its humiliation in humanity:

> The appearance of man-gods, sharing the passions and joys of men who are purely men, is certainly a common characteristic of pagan poems. But in paganism, as the price for this manifestation, the gods lose their divinity. Hence philosophers expel poets from the City to preserve the divinity of the gods in men's minds. But divinity thus saved lacks all condescension.... Infinity then manifests itself *in* the finite, but it does not manifest itself *to* the finite.[23]

In paganism, the gods either remain entirely transcendent to the concerns of man or lose their divinity in being rendered immanent to the world of men (the city). This maintains the order of man, placing divinity either firmly outside the city as divine or inside as just another man, which precludes the possibility of divine revelation to man. The Christian doctrine of kenosis, meanwhile, disrupts this order by providing a new way of relating to transcendence: a god who is God precisely in being man, whose transcendence lies in condescension, whose glory exists in humiliation. God's humiliation—his coming down to our level in order to raise us up to his—allows us to conceive of transcendence, not as what *breaks into* immanence from *beyond*, but as what *opens up* immanence from *within*:

---

22. Ward, *Christ and Culture*, 196; see 189–98 for context.
23. Levinas, *Entre Nous*, 54; emphasis in original.

> The idea of a truth whose manifestation is not glorious or bursting with light, the idea of a truth that manifests itself in its humility, like the still small voice in the biblical expression—the idea of a persecuted truth—is that not henceforth the only possible modality of transcendence? . . . To manifest itself as humble, as allied with the vanquished, the poor, the persecuted—is precisely not to return to the order. . . . To present oneself in this poverty of the exile is to interrupt the coherence of the universe. To pierce immanence without thereby taking one's place within it. Obviously such an opening can only be an ambiguity.[24]

The ambiguity is the paradox of God's power in weakness, transcendence in immanence, divinity in humanity: "The ambiguity of transcendence," Levinas says, is not "a failure of the intelligence that examines it" or "the feeble faith surviving the death of God," but "precisely the proximity of God which can only occur in humility" as "the original mode of the presence of God, the original mode of communication."[25]

An example of the fact that Levinas sees Paul's kenosis as speaking to a set of problems far broader than Christology is his remarkable essay "Judaism and Kenosis." It uncovers Levinas's understanding of kenosis in the kabbalistic cosmology of the nineteenth-century Lithuanian rabbi Chaim of Volozhin. The rabbi presents God's reign over creation as requiring ethical mediation through human action: "God associates with or withdraws from the worlds, depending upon human behaviour. Man is answerable for the universe! Man is answerable for others."[26] Or, more specifically:

> This is the ethical meaning of human activity: . . . God's reign depends on me. . . . God reigns only by the intermediary of an ethical order, an order in which one being is answerable for another. The world *is*, not because it perseveres in being, not because *being* is its own *raison d'être*, but because, through the human enterprise, it can be justified in its being. . . . More important than God's omnipotence is the subordination of that power to man's ethical consent. And that, too, is one of the primordial meanings of kenosis.[27]

Levinas sees this as kenosis because it understands God in terms of weakness, unequal to divinity, emphasizes the order of the finite human being's

---

24. Levinas, *Entre Nous*, 55.
25. Levinas, *Entre Nous*, 56.
26. Levinas, *In the Time*, 125.
27. Levinas, *In the Time*, 126; emphasis in original.

actions in the world down below: "This God, master of power, is powerless to associate himself with the world he creates . . . and maintains in being by that very association, without a certain behaviour of man," which consequently ensures that "everything depends on man," for "the vocation, or *raison d'être*, of humanity is precisely to provide the necessary conditions for the association of God with the worlds, and thus for the being of the worlds."[28] Likewise, in Christianity, God becomes human for the sake of his revelation to and reconciliation with humanity. Kenosis thus emphasizes man as what Renée van Riessen, in her study of the kenotic motif in Levinas, has called "a place of God." She explains: "Kenosis is the event in which God makes room for human action. Conversely, for Levinas, the human being is 'a place of God.' Its existence is meaningful as a reference to the kenotic God, in the devotional movement of 'À Dieu.'"[29] Since God has come down to the level of humanity, the human being becomes the site where divinity takes place. "Paradoxically," Levinas therefore concludes, "everything depends on them—those whose bodies are at the lowest level, located within the order of action and work, at the level of matter. Everything depends on them, even the outpouring of God,"[30] since "to some degree, in relation to the human will, the Divine is then subordinate. There is kenosis in this 'sub-.'"[31]

Vattimo's Metaphysical Kenosis

Levinas still understands his philosophical analysis of kenosis as ultimately being completed by a theological one: he merely wants "to show the points beyond which nothing can replace religion."[32] However, in his *Belief*, Gianni Vattimo proposes something far more radical: by centring its theology around kenosis, Christianity de-theologizes or secularizes itself in a movement he calls *weakening*. For Vattimo, like for Levinas, kenosis introduces a new relation to transcendence, namely as to be found down below within, rather than beyond or above, the world: "The guiding thread of Jesus' interpretation of the Old Testament is the new and more profound relation of charity established between God and humanity, and consequently between

28. Levinas, *In the Time*, 122.
29. Van Riessen, *Man as Place of God*, 12.
30. Levinas, *In the Time*, 124 (translation modified).
31. Levinas, *In the Time*, 122.
32. Levinas, *Entre Nous*, 54.

human beings themselves,"[33] meaning "that the 'kenotic' interpretation of the articles of faith goes hand in hand with the life of every person," namely "the commitment to transform them into concrete principles that are incarnate in one's own existence, and irreducible to a formula."[34]

However, Vattimo goes further and suggests that the kenotic doctrine of God actually effaces theological transcendence altogether: "The only great paradox and scandal of Christian revelation is the incarnation of God, the kenosis—that is, the removal of all the transcendent, incomprehensible, mysterious and even bizarre features," at least when this transcendence is understood in "a naturalistic, human, all too human, ultimately unchristian" way (i.e., metaphysically).[35] Transcendence is thus not merely related to differently, it is understood differently, namely kenotically. However, crucially, it is Christianity itself, with its kenotic doctrine of God, that establishes this understanding of divine transcendence as its own effacement: the gesture characteristic of Christianity is to efface divine transcendence, what Nancy calls "de-theologization" and Vattimo calls "secularization."

Vattimo then presents us with a "Christianity recovered as the doctrine of salvation (namely, secularizing kenosis)."[36] He explains:

> Salvation is an event in which kenosis, the abasement of God, is realized more and more fully and so undermines the wisdom of the world, the metaphysical dreams of natural reason which conceive God as absolute, omnipotent and transcendent, *ipsum esse (metaphysicum) subsistens*. In this light, secularization—the progressive dissolution of the natural sacred—is the very essence of Christianity.[37]

De-theologization or "secularization as the essence of modernity and of Christianity itself," thus means a weakening of the metaphysical structures in which Christianity articulated itself along with its theology—i.e., their self-effacement or self-emptying—since at its core sits the secularizing "feature of kenosis in which the history of salvation is realized" and "must be attributed to this whole experience of 'dissolution', or the weakening of strong structures."[38] This gesture does not oppose itself to "Christianity" or

33. Vattimo, *Belief*, 49.
34. Vattimo, *Belief*, 72.
35. Vattimo, *Belief*, 55.
36. Vattimo, *Belief*, 62.
37. Vattimo, *Belief*, 49–50.
38. Vattimo, *Belief*, 52.

"theology," but instead opens a new Christianity or theology, wrests itself away from a supposedly contingent metaphysical framework. Crucially, however, this movement *beyond* "Christianity" (onto-theology) precisely *starts from* Christianity itself (the kenosis of God). Tracing this movement is the task Nancy's deconstruction of Christianity sets itself.

Nancy's Cultural Kenosis

In the preamble to his two-volume project entitled *The Deconstruction of Christianity*, Jean-Luc Nancy states his intentions: "It is not our concern to save religion, even less to return to it. The much discussed 'return of the religious,' which denotes a real phenomenon, deserves no more attention than any other 'return.'"[39] If Nancy's deconstruction of Christianity forms his own turn to religion, it does not aim at a return to the religious or theological mode of thought. Instead, his question concerns something entirely different: Nancy is interested in a resource, found *within* Christianity, carrying us *beyond* Christianity: as the religion of the egress of religion, Christianity carries within itself the gesture of its own self-surpassing.[40] The deconstruction of Christianity concerns itself with precisely that gesture:

> My question will be very simple, naïve even, as is perhaps fitting at the beginning of a phenomenological procedure: How and to what degree do *we hold* to Christianity? How, exactly, are we, in our whole tradition, held by it? . . . Christianity itself, Christianity *as such*, is surpassed. That state of self-surpassing may be very profoundly proper to it; it is perhaps its deepest tradition. . . . It is this transcendence, this going-beyond-itself that must therefore be examined.[41]

This gesture of Christianity's self-surpassing—one that *starts from* Christianity yet *moves beyond* Christianity—is envisioned by the deconstruction of Christianity as "the operation consisting in disassembling the elements that constitute it, in order to attempt to discern, among these elements and as if behind them, that which made their assembly possible,"[42] in order to "go back to (or to advance toward) a resource that could form at once the buried origin and the imperceptible future of the world that calls itself

---

39. Nancy, *Dis-Enclosure*, 1.
40. Nancy, *Dis-Enclosure*, 34.
41. Nancy, *Dis-Enclosure*, 139–41; emphasis in original.
42. Nancy, *Dis-Enclosure*, 32.

'modern.'"[43] If we understand deconstruction as the gesture of taking apart a complex whole in order to discover what makes it fit together, only to find that once taken apart it cannot be put together anymore, we find that, on Nancy's account, deconstruction is identified with Christianity itself in its movement of self-surpassing: what is characteristic of Christianity moves us beyond Christianity as the agent of its own secularization or de-theologization. Indeed, "the gesture of deconstruction," Nancy says, "is itself shot through and through with Christianity," and is therefore "only possible within Christianity."[44] Consequently, the deconstruction of Christianity is a self-deconstruction: deconstruction is not something done to Christianity from without, but something going on within the Christian religion as its very Christianity. Nancy's core claim is that Christianity *is* nothing but this movement, this deconstruction, this de-theologization or secularization, of itself as itself.[45] In short, Christianity is Christian in its own "de-Christianization" or self-deconstruction: "Deconstruction . . . is itself Christian . . . because Christianity is, originally, deconstructive. . . . *The structure of origin of Christianity is the proclamation of its end.*"[46]

We can already anticipate where in Christianity Nancy will find its self-deconstructive agent—the origin that proclaims its end—namely its kenotic doctrine of God: like the Christian God is God only in his self-effacement as "God" (the form), Christianity is Christian only in its self-effacement as "Christianity" (the religion). However, before exploring Nancy's treatment of the kenotic motif and his development of the deconstruction of Christianity, it is worth contextualizing this project. We should understand it in the context of an essay by a friend and collaborator of Nancy's, namely Jean-Christophe Bailly's *Adieu*. In his meditation on the meaning of the death of God, Bailly insightfully remarks that "farewell [*adieu*] has not really been said to God [*à Dieu*]. He is no longer there, that's all."[47] Specifically, "modern Western man did not really want the death of God, he has simply lost God along the way [*en route*], and in such a foolish way that he has not even realised it yet."[48] This is a perfect summary of Nietzsche's development of this idea, where a "madman" (who nevertheless "lit a lantern in the bright

43. Nancy, *Dis-Enclosure*, 34.
44. Nancy, *Dis-Enclosure*, 148.
45. Nancy, *Dis-Enclosure*, 35.
46. Nancy, *Dis-Enclosure*, 149; emphasis in original.
47. Bailly, *Adieu*, 16.
48. Bailly, *Adieu*, 33.

morning hours"), urgently proclaims the death of God, not to the believers, but to the cultured despisers who think to have no need of him. Yet, they do not listen for they do not understand what they have done, they do not comprehend the consequences of this death they themselves nevertheless accomplished.[49] It is with this tremendous, and indeed still ongoing, event that Bailly wants to come to grips by making its extensive reverberations felt. Or, as he puts it: "Truly saying farewell [*adieu*] . . . to God [*à Dieu*]."[50] This cannot be done in an instant, merely noting the death is insufficient; it requires a laborious effort of bidding God farewell: not merely writing his obituary, but clearing out his house and selling off his possessions—deconstructing the various constructions secured by him. In other words, we need to perform the work of mourning his death: "I propose that thinking what 'God is dead' means and doing the work of mourning are one and the same thing."[51] The work of mourning God's death is an intellectual labor: thinking through the effects of the death of God, the erasure of the horizon, the unchaining of the earth from its sun. It means considering the meaning of a *genuine atheism*, which is not merely a denial of God (anti-theism), but something much more difficult: ceasing any reference to God (a-theism). Atheism, Bailly suggests, means "saying simply that which is, the world shines in the absence of God, any god, it shines *divinely* in this absence."[52] That is the *challenge* the death of God poses to thought, to be met only in the intellectual labor of mourning this death.

Nancy's deconstruction undertakes precisely this work of mourning: it is not an accomplishment (i.e., achieving a "deconstructed Christianity" resembling C. S. Lewis's "mere Christianity"), but the project or endeavor of *bidding farewell to God* (i.e., tracking Christianity in its self-deconstruction). Rather than Christianity, Nancy's question therefore concerns the possibility of a genuine atheism: thinking in the wake of the death of God. He nevertheless finds the answer in Christianity, precisely because it has made the death of God into a religion: "Only an atheism that contemplates the reality of its Christian provenance can be actual."[53] That Christian provenance points the way towards a genuine atheism, namely a world without any reference to God, a world without given meaning other than its own

49. Nietzsche, *Gay Science*, 181–82.
50. Bailly, *Adieu*, 10.
51. Bailly, *Adieu*, 17.
52. Bailly, *Adieu*, 18–19; emphasis in original.
53. Nancy, *Dis-Enclosure*, 140 (author's translation).

being-world.[54] Thinking the world without God, thinking atheologically or *moving beyond* theology, is Nancy's project. Yet, he says, it must be done precisely by *starting from* Christianity itself, the de-theologization going on within it, the self-deconstruction that it is. This is what it means to bid farewell to God, to carry out the work of mourning his death, to de-theologize thought—indeed, to deconstruct Christianity. If we were to apply this to contemporary phenomenology, as I will now argue that we must, we could equally say that this is what it means to think *after the theological turn*, namely to let phenomenology de-theologize itself.

DECONSTRUCTING THE THEOLOGICAL TURN

After the theological turn, what is next for Continental philosophy of religion? Or more precisely, what can it mean to think *after the theological turn* in terms of the phenomenological method that is precisely at issue in that turn? My proposal is that it is time to engage, phenomenologically, with the authors of the "kenotic turn" in an attempt at spelling out the full consequences of the theological turn phenomenology took at the end of the previous century: insofar as Christian theology's kenotic logic dictates that any turn towards theology eventually results in a movement beyond it, that movement remains unthought by the former as a question of phenomenology. In other words, another deconstruction announces itself: neither of phenomenology (Derrida), nor of Christianity (Nancy), but of phenomenology's theological turn. Here, I propose that this project can be pursued as what I would somewhat paradoxically call *phenomenology of kenosis*.

Curiously, the authors of kenotic turn are rarely studied in relation to phenomenology's theological turn, presumably because these respective movements proceed in opposite directions. The question therefore arises whether the return of religion really is a unified phenomenon. Assuming that it is, as the scholarship does, an account of how the theological turn relates to the kenotic turn is required: What do these two diverging movements, *taken together*, give us to think? Well, if the *theological turn* exemplifies how philosophy (and phenomenology in particular) turns (in) to theology (e.g., by taking the revelation of Christ as paradigm for experience generally); and if the *kenotic turn* shows how Christianity exists in a movement of self-effacement or de-theologization (e.g., by depicting God's self-emptying of divinity in the incarnation as setting in motion

54. Nancy, *Dis-Enclosure*, 35.

Christianity's self-deconstruction); then I would suggest that the *return of religion* is the movement in which philosophy (and phenomenology in particular), precisely in and only by turning to theology, de-theologizes itself. If the Word must assume a condition foreign to itself (humanity) in order to come to itself (Jesus Christ as incarnate divinity), then philosophy must turn to theology in order to properly understand itself in its atheological bearing. In short, by thinking *after the theological turn*, I mean a deconstruction or de-theologization of phenomenology's inherent theological structure as a movement *beyond*, though *starting from*, the theological turn it facilitated: a phenomenology that does not straightforwardly turn into theology, that has been de-theologized, is best equipped to account for religious or theophanic experience *phenomenologically* (i.e., an account that is not itself "theological").

This parallels the project Derrida undertakes in his final book, *On Touching—Jean-Luc Nancy*, an extensive study of his friend's work: reprising his earlier critique of phenomenology as always oriented towards an impossible, immediate, and auto-affective presence by way of a comprehensive deconstruction of Husserl's "principle of all principles," he suggests that phenomenology's structural problems are exacerbated when it comes into contact with Christianity, as it does in phenomenology's theological turn.[55] Whereas Derrida concerns himself primarily with Husserl, it is worth taking up that same deconstruction in reference to Husserl's theologizing French interpreters. However, here too, everything still depends on what Husserl understands as the principle of phenomenology, namely that its field of study is intuition as it is *leibhaftig gegeben* (literally "bodily given"). or "given in its personal actuality" (its usual idiomatic English translation).[56] Phenomenology is the study of the appearing of things *in propria persona*, letting them appear as they give themselves out to be: "to let what shows itself be seen from itself," Heidegger says, "just as it shows itself from itself."[57] Yet, everything turns on how the German is translated. In France (and Italy), the translation lends itself easily to theologizing: namely, *givenness in the flesh* (*en chair, in carne*). This Gallicism inscribes the potential for a theological turn (i.e., towards *sarx*) within phenomenology from the outset by overdetermining the meaning of its principle, thereby allowing for example Didier Franck to speak of *incarnate givenness*, which

---

55. See Derrida, *On Touching*.
56. Husserl, *Ideas*, 44; Heidegger, *Being and Time*, 318; Derrida, *On the Name*, 236.
57. Heidegger, *Being and Time*, 30.

Marion identifies with *revelation*.⁵⁸ Take the opening lines of Marion's Gifford lectures, entitled *Givenness and Revelation*: "This title may . . . surprise," he says, "nothing seems to join an apparently old and steadfastly theological notion together with a philosophical concept drawn from the most recent phenomenology. However, if we want wanted to consider better their respective features, the two terms could instead converge."⁵⁹ For Marion and his colleagues, the philosophical and theological converge in or as phenomenology, in philosophy's (re)turn to religion. In short, phenomenology facilitates a *theologization of philosophy* by placing the terms proper to each discipline on the same axis as *phenomenologically* synonymous. Specifically, the theological turn understands: (1) givenness (*Gegebenheit*) along the lines of revelation; (2) embodiment (*Leiblichkeit*) along the lines of incarnation; and (thereby), (3) phenomenological philosophy along the lines of revealed theology. Derrida observed that this is due to the structural tendency of phenomenology itself, which makes its turn to theology possible in principle; yet, these structural tendencies are exacerbated, and manifested particularly acutely, when phenomenology explicitly entertains the Christian understanding of revelation or incarnation, as it does in its actual theological turn.

A deconstruction of phenomenology's theological turn therefore claims the following: when exploring philosophy's theologization in phenomenology's theological turn, facilitated by the *apparent* convergence of philosophical and theological notions in the basic terms of phenomenology; we discover that these notions *in fact* diverge in the way they expose phenomenology's structural problems, thereby de-theologizing philosophy and even de-Christianizing phenomenology (i.e., making evident the divergence). In other words, a deconstructive approach to the authors of the theological turn might demonstrate how they incorrectly place philosophical and theological terms on the same axis, regarding them as phenomenologically synonymous: (1) givenness cannot be thought along the lines of revelation (against Marion); (2) embodiment cannot be thought along the lines of incarnation (against Henry); and (therefore), (3) phenomenological philosophy cannot be thought along the lines of revealed theology. Only once established that *Gegebenheit* does not mean the revelation of Christ, and that *Leiblichkeit* does not mean the incarnation of God (i.e., only once phenomenology is de-theologized), can we appreciate the

---

58. See respectively Franck, *Flesh and Body*; Marion, *Visible and Revealed*.
59. Marion, *Givenness and Revelation*, 1.

properly *phenomenological* meaning of these terms (i.e., as distinct from their theological resonance—which, it cannot be stressed enough, they lack *entirely* in German).

Like Derrida's engagement with Husserl, this would not be a critique coming from without, but a deconstruction going on within that it would be a matter of documenting: it is a question of exposing how the shortcomings of the existing phenomenological accounts are due to the inherent play of contradiction and displacement within their basic assumptions. In short, *thinking after the theological turn* means showing how the *phenomenological coupling* of philosophical (givenness and embodiment) and theological terms (revelation and incarnation) *deconstructs itself* within that turn. Only by delving into phenomenology's turn *towards* theology (the texts and language of the Christian tradition), does the kenotic turn then show us how to turn *away* from "the theological" (the metaphysical priority of transcendence): to de-theologize philosophy. Thinking *after the theological turn*, purging philosophy of "theology," can then only be done by exploring its inherently theological structure, precisely by taking a *kenotic turn*.

CONCLUSION

By outlining what I have called the "kenotic turn," I have demonstrated how the challenge of contemporary Continental philosophy of religion is to think "after the theological turn," to deconstruct the theological turn by critically engaging the state in which it has left the field rather than forever continuing to "turn" (undoubtedly in circles) in what would amount to a new form of scholasticism. In that sense, "phenomenology is not a school," as Heidegger reminds us, but merely denotes "the possibility of thinking" as "corresponding to the claim of what is to be thought."[60] Today, it is indeed still the theological turn that demands to be thought but only insofar as it has been completed (only a single one of its authors still being alive): the turn has been taken and it is now time to look ahead towards where the road might take us next as well as to look back in the rearview mirror to see how exactly we ended up where we are (in the ditch of theology, as Janicaud insisted).[61]

The proposal I have put forward here, or at least the direction I hope to give for any future turn phenomenology might take following this first

60. Heidegger, *On Time and Being*, 82.
61. Janicaud, "Theological Turn."

(theological) step, centered on the theological notion of kenosis and its role as a Christian metaphor for deconstruction within contemporary Continental philosophy. In other words, I have suggested that "thinking after the theological turn" concerns the deconstruction of the theological structure inherent to phenomenology in principle and manifested acutely by its actual theological turn: namely, by *starting from* the theological turn phenomenology was structurally inclined to produce, *moving beyond* theology as such. Phenomenology must thus take it upon itself to bid farewell (*adieu*) to God (*à Dieu*), must undertake the work of mourning his death, by engaging in what I proposed to call a "phenomenology of kenosis." We might then say that after "the theological turn of recent phenomenology" (a turn *towards theology*) could come "the kenotic turn of contemporary phenomenology" (a turn *away from theology* but precisely following and only *on the basis of* the earlier turn): today, phenomenology must indeed turn to theology, but only to discover therein what is properly speaking "phenomenological" by immediately also moving beyond "the theological"—as an instance of what Emmanuel Falque, who is arguably the first philosopher to think "after the theological turn" in this way, has insightfully referred to as the "backlash" of theology on phenomenology.[62] It is the Christian theological notion of kenosis, which captures the meaning of God as the very effacement of the *theos*, that provides phenomenology with the opportunity to do just that, to de-theologize itself precisely by feeling the backlash of theology.

BIBLIOGRAPHY

Agamben, Giorgio. *The Time That Remains: A Commentary on the Letter to the Romans*. Translated by Patricia Dailey. Stanford, CA: Stanford University Press, 2005.

Alexandrova, Alena, et al. "Re-Opening the Question of Religion: Dis-Enclosure of Religion and Modernity in the Philosophy of Jean-Luc Nancy." In *Re-Treating Religion: Deconstructing Christianity with Jean-Luc Nancy*, edited by Alena Alexandrova et al., 22–40. Perspectives in Continental Philosophy. New York: Fordham University Press, 2012.

———, eds. *Re-Treating Religion: Deconstructing Christianity with Jean-Luc Nancy*. Perspectives in Continental Philosophy. New York: Fordham University Press, 2012.

Badiou, Alain. *Saint Paul: The Foundation of Universalism*. Translated by Ray Brassier. Cultural Memory in the Present. Stanford, CA: Stanford University Press, 2003.

Bailly, Jean-Christophe. *Adieu: Essai sur la mort des dieux*. Paris: Defaut, 2014.

Baird, Marie L. "Whose *Kenosis*? An Analysis of Levinas, Derrida, and Vattimo on God's Self-Emptying and the Secularisation of the West." *HeyJ* 48 (2007) 423–37.

---

62. Falque: *Crossing the Rubicon*, 149–50; *Loving Struggle*, 172.

PART I. KENOSIS IN POLITICAL THEOLOGY

Blond, Philip, ed. *Post-Secular Philosophy: Between Philosophy and Theology*. London: Routledge, 1997.

Caputo, John D. "The Hyperbolization of Phenomenology: Two Possibilities for Religion in Recent Continental Philosophy." In *Counter-Experiences: Reading Jean-Luc Marion*, edited by Kevin Hart, 67–94. Notre Dame, IN: University of Notre Dame Press, 2007.

———. *The Prayers and Tears of Jacques Derrida: Religion Without Religion*. Bloomington: Indiana University Press, 1997.

———. *The Weakness of God: A Theology of the Event*. Bloomington: Indiana University Press, 2006.

Cassidy-Deketelaere, Nikolaas. *Jean-Luc Nancy After the Theological Turn: A Phenomenology of Kenosis*. London: Bloomsbury, 2025.

Courtine, Jean-François, ed. *Phénoménologie et théologie*. Paris: Criterion, 1992.

Crockett, Clayton, et al., eds. *The Future of Continental Philosophy of Religion*. Bloomington: Indiana University Press, 2014.

Dawe, Donald. G. *The Form of a Servant: A Historical Analysis of the Kenotic Motif*. Philadelphia: Westminster, 1964.

Derrida, Jacques. *On the Name*. Edited by Thomas Dutoit. Translated by David Wood. Stanford, CA: Stanford University Press, 1995.

———. *On Touching—Jean-Luc Nancy*. Translated by Christine Irizarry. Stanford, CA: Stanford University Press, 2005.

De Vries, Hent. *Philosophy and the Turn to Religion*. Baltimore: Johns Hopkins University Press, 1999.

De Vries, Hent, and Lawrence E. Sullivan, eds. *Political Theologies: Public Religions in a Post-Secular World*. New York: Fordham University Press, 2006.

Dubilet, Alex. *The Self-Emptying Subject: Kenosis and Immanence, Medieval to Modern*. New York: Fordham University Press, 2018.

Falque, Emmanuel. *Crossing the Rubicon: The Borderlands of Philosophy and Theology*. Translated by Reuben Shank. New York: Fordham University Press, 2016.

———. *The Metamorphosis of Finitude: An Essay on Birth and Resurrection*. Translated by George Hughes. New York: Fordham University Press, 2012.

Franck, Didier. *Flesh and Body: On the Phenomenology of Husserl*, Translated by Joseph Rivera and Scott Davidson. London: Bloomsbury, 2014.

Habermas, Jürgen. *Between Naturalism and Religion: Philosophical Essays*. Translated by Ciaran Cronin. Cambridge: Polity, 2008.

Hegel, G. W. F. *The Phenomenology of Spirit*. Translated by A. V. Miller. Oxford: Oxford University Press, 1977.

Heidegger, Martin. *Being and Time*. Translated by Joan Stambaugh. Revised by Dennis J. Schmidt. Albany: SUNY Press, 2010.

———. *On Time and Being*. Translated by Joan Stambaugh. Chicago: University of Chicago Press, 2002.

Henry, Michel. *Incarnation: A Philosophy of Flesh*. Translated by Karl Hefty. Studies in Phenomenology and Existential Philosophy. Evanston: Northwestern University Press, 2015.

Husserl, Edmund. *Ideas Pertaining to a Pure Phenomenology and to a Phenomenological Philosophy—First Book: General Introduction to a Pure Phenomenology*. Translated by F. Kersten. Vol. 2 of *Husserliana: Edmund Husserl—Collected Works*. The Hague: Nijhoff, 1982.

Hutchens, B. C. *Jean-Luc Nancy and the Future of Philosophy*. Montreal: McGill-Queen's University Press, 2005.

James, Ian. "Incarnation and Infinity." In *Re-Treating Religion: Deconstructing Christianity with Jean-Luc Nancy*, edited by Alena Alexandrova et al., 246–60. Perspectives in Continental Philosophy. New York: Fordham University Press, 2012.

———. *The New French Philosophy*. Cambridge: Polity, 2012.

Janicaud, Dominique. *La phénoménologie dans tous ses états*. Folio essais 514. Paris: Gallimard, 2009.

———. "The Theological Turn in French Phenomenology." In *Phenomenology and the "Theological Turn": The French Debate*, translated by Bernard G. Prusak, 1–103. New York: Fordham University Press, 2000.

Lambert, Gregg. *Return Statements: The Return of Religion in Contemporary Philosophy*. Incitements. Edinburgh: Edinburgh University Press, 2016.

Latré, Stijn, et al., eds. *Radical Secularisation? An Inquiry into the Religious Roots of Secular Culture*. London: Bloomsbury, 2014.

Levinas, Emmanuel. *Entre Nous: Thinking-of-the-Other*. Translated by Michael B. Smith and Barbara Harshav. New York: Columbia University Press, 1998.

———. *In the Time of Nations*. Translated by Michael B. Smith. Bloomington: Indiana University Press, 1994.

———. *Of God Who Comes to Mind*. Translated by Bettina Bergo. Stanford, CA: Stanford University Press, 1998.

Marion, Jean-Luc. *Givenness and Revelation*. Translated by Stephen E. Lewis. Oxford: Oxford University Press, 2016.

———. *The Visible and the Revealed*. Translated by Christina M. Gschwandtner et al. New York: Fordham University Press, 2008.

McLennan, Gregor. "The Postsecular Turn." *Theory, Culture & Society* 27 (2010) 3–20.

Milbank, John, et al., eds. *Radical Orthodoxy: A New Theology*. Routledge Radical Orthodoxy. London: Routledge, 1999.

Nancy, Jean-Luc. *Adoration*. Vol. 2 of *The Deconstruction of Christianity*. Translated by John McKeane. New York: Fordham University Press, 2012.

———. *Dis-Enclosure*. Vol. 1 of *The Deconstruction of Christianity*. Translated by Gabriel Malenfant et al. New York: Fordham University Press, 2008.

———. "Entzug der Göttlichkeit: Zur Dekonstruktion und Selbstüberschreitung des Christentums." *Lettre International* 59 (2002) 76–80.

———. *Expectation: Philosophy, Literature*. Translated by Robert Bononno. New York: Fordham University Press, 2017.

———. *The Inoperative Community*. Translated by Peter Connor et al. Minneapolis: Minnesota University Press, 1991.

Nietzsche, Friedrich. *The Gay Science*. Translated by Walter Kaufmann. New York: Vintage, 1974.

Smith, Anthony Paul, and Daniel Whistler, eds. *After the Postsecular and the Postmodern: New Essays in Continental Philosophy of Religion*. Cambridge: Cambridge University Press, 2010.

Smith, James K. A. "Liberating Religion from Theology: Marion and Heidegger on the Possibility of a Phenomenology of Religion." *International Journal for Philosophy of Religion* 46 (1999) 17–23.

Staudigl, Michael, and Jason W. Alvis, eds. *Phenomenology and the Post-Secular Turn: Contemporary Debates on the "Return of Religion."* London: Routledge, 2018.

PART I. KENOSIS IN POLITICAL THEOLOGY

Van Riessen, Renée D. N. *Man as a Place of God: Levinas' Hermeneutics of Kenosis*. Amsterdam Studies in Jewish Philosophy 13. Dordrecht: Springer, 2007.
Vattimo, Gianni. *Belief.* Translated by Luca D'Istano. Cambridge: Polity, 1999.
Vial, Marc. "Dieu jusque dans le néant: Sur la kénose." *RHPR* 95 (2015) 339–57.
Ward, Graham. *Christ and Culture*. Oxford: Blackwell, 2005.
Watkin, Christopher. *Difficult Atheism: Post-Theological Thinking in Alain Badiou, Jean-Luc Nancy and Quentin Meillassoux*. Crosscurrents. Edinburgh: Edinburgh University Press, 2011.
Zijlstra, Onno, ed. *Letting Go: Rethinking Kenosis*. Bern: Lang, 2002.
Žižek, Slavoj. *The Puppet and the Dwarf: The Perverse Core of Christianity*. Cambridge, MA: MIT Press, 2003.

PART II.

Kenosis in the Kyoto School and the Non-Western Tradition

5

A Hidden Japanese Source of Kenosis in Contemporary Christian Theology?

Kyoto School, Kazo Kitamori, and Jürgen Moltmann

Yusuke Okada

1. INTRODUCTION: A HIDDEN JAPANESE SOURCE OF KENOSIS?

In recent scholarship, one can observe the rise of *global history* as a general methodology of the humanities.[1] Although the narratives of history as a modern discipline of the humanities required its objective rigidity, it was more or less influenced by the hidden Eurocentrism, in which the West was always placed as the center of the narratives of universal history. Challenging this tendency, the methodology of global history attempts to correct the prevailing Eurocentrism by relativizing the status of the West as a mere province of the globe and by valuing the contributions of non-European actors. Ideas and innovations were not only brought by Europeans or the

---

1. The Work of C. A. Bayly is regarded as a classic of global history: *Birth of Modern World*. See also Conrad, *What Is Global History?*; Moyn and Sartori, *Global Intellectual History*.

West, but were formed in intercultural exchange on a global scale. Following this method, this contribution seeks to apply the narrative of global history to the topic of this volume, reevaluating one of the hidden sources of kenosis in contemporary Christian theology.

In the history of contemporary theology, the German systematic theologian Jürgen Moltmann (1926–2024) played an important role in the rediscovery and reevaluation of kenosis as a central idea of Christian ethics. Although he does not use the term kenosis so explicitly, his seminal work, *The Crucified God*, as one of the programmatic books of his political theology, elaborated the kenotic motif as the symbol of his political theology. Moltmann's kenotic theology, however, is not a product of a purely "Western" or "European" culture, but a product of a globally entangled intellectual history. In a passage of *The Crucified God*, Moltmann refers to a Japanese theologian named Kazoh Kitamori and writes as follows:

> At about the same time [of D. Bonhoeffer], and in a similar political situation in his country, the Japanese Lutheran theologian Kazoh Kitamori was writing his book *Theology of the Pain of God*, in which he developed a similar theology of the cross: the pain of God heals our pains. In the suffering of Christ God himself suffers. These suggestions must be taken further.[2]

Referring to Kitamori's *Theology of the Pain of God*, Moltmann argues that the idea of God's pain and suffering has great resonance with his political theology and that this idea needs to be developed further. Although Kazoh Kitamori and his theology of the pain of God are not as famous or popular today as they were a few decades ago, Kitamori is still, mainly because of this reference by Moltmann, probably one of the best-known Japanese theologians in the context of intercultural theology.[3] Of course, this does not mean that Kitamori's theology had a decisive influence on the formation of Moltmann's theology. Surely Moltmann could have written *The Crucified God* without reference to Kitamori's theology of God's suffering. Nevertheless, it is an interesting phenomenon that theologians from different cultural backgrounds used the similar motif of kenosis to express their theology in the time of crisis in the second half of the twentieth century.

---

2. Moltmann, *Crucified God*, 47.

3. Anri Morimoto names, for example, Kazoh Kitamori, Toyohiko Kagawa, and Kosuke Koyama ("3 Ks") as the most internationally well-known Japanese theologians, contrasting them to the "3 Bs" as the German counterpart (Karl Barth, Rudolf Bultmann, and Emil Brunner) (Morimoto, "Editor's Preface").

In this sense, Moltmann's reference to Kitamori can be seen as a symbolic intercultural intersection of the idea of kenosis in contemporary theology.

With regard to the interculturality of the idea of kenosis, it is also worth noting that Kitamori has the background of the Kyoto School. The Kyoto School is the network of scholars around its key figures such as Kitaro Nishida and Hajime Tanabe at Kyoto University.[4] The core of its philosophy can be ideal-typically characterized as a reinterpretation of Mahāyāna Buddhist teachings with the conceptuality of modern Western philosophy, such as German classical philosophy or phenomenology. The philosophy of the Kyoto School is especially well known in the field of intercultural and interreligious dialogue between Buddhism and Christianity because of its clear, philosophical, and modern conceptualization of Buddhist ideas as well as its harsh criticism of Christianity based on its deep understanding.[5] Although Kitamori is not usually considered a member of the Kyoto School, he studied with Tanabe at the University of Kyoto,[6] and his theology can be partially interpreted as a response to Nishida's critique of Christian theology. Therefore, in order to deepen the interculturality of the idea of kenosis, it should be worthwhile to dig into the Kyoto School–Kitamori–Moltmann line in order to highlight a hidden Japanese source of kenosis in contemporary Christian theology.[7]

2. NISHIDA KITARO: KENOSIS AS THE ONTOLOGICAL AND METAPHYSICAL STATUS OF THE ABSOLUTE

In order to see the influence of the Kyoto School on Kitamori, this study begins with Nishida Kitaro's philosophy of religion. Although Kitamori studied under Tanabe's instruction, he later recalled that he concentrated

---

4. For this definition, see Takeda, *Story of "Kyoto School,"* 388.

5. Regarding the Kyoto School in the context of Buddhism-Christianity dialogue, see Brück and Lai, *Buddhismus und Christentum*.

6. Kitamori, "In Memory of Prof. Tanabe."

7. Before beginning the description, it is necessary to recall that this study does not insist on a strong causality between them, as if the preceding thinker was the necessary condition for the following one. Kitamori would have been able to write his *Theology of the Pain of God* without the influence of the Kyoto School. Moltmann would (certainly) have been able to write his theology of the crucified God without Kitamori's theology. Nevertheless, tracing the loose connection between the Kyoto School, Kitamori, and Moltmann will contribute to the global intertwining that has recently been highly valued in the field of global intellectual history.

on studying Nishida's philosophy during his time as a student, suggesting that the basic structure of his theology was constructed as a response to Nishida's later criticism of Christianity.[8] Moreover, Nishida himself uses the idea of kenosis in his philosophy of religion, but in a way that differs greatly from the original use of the term in Christian theology. To contrast the idea of kenosis between the Kyoto School and Kitamori, this section analyzes Nishida's philosophy, especially his later philosophy of religion in "The Logic of Place and Religious Worldview."[9]

The fundamental principle of Nishida's philosophy of religion is the concept of the Absolute, which is conceived in contrast to its antonym, the relative: On the one hand, beings are relative when they are related and comparable to each other. For example, Nishida and Kitamori are relative beings in that they are both human beings. Kitamori is younger than Nishida, and they are in an academic relationship insofar as Kitamori is influenced by Nishida, and Kitamori tries to answer Nishida's criticism of Christianity. The beings that are in relation to others and in confrontation with others are all understood as relative beings.

On the other hand, the Absolute cannot be compared or related to other beings on the same level. By its very definition, it must exist independently and transcend any relativity. Nishida illustrates his idea by using Japanese terms for the relative and the Absolute:[10] The relative is translated into Japanese as *Sōtai* (相対), which consists of two Chinese characters and roughly means "pairs" or "confrontation." As in a dialogue over a coffee table or a confrontation between two chess players, the Japanese terms for the relative have the connotation of two opponents on the same level standing or sitting against each other. On the other hand, the Absolute is translated into Japanese as *Zettai* (絶対), which literally means "to destroy the opponent" or "to annihilate the opponent." The Absolute does not or cannot enter into a relationship with other beings from the beginning, because it destroys and annihilates the confronting opponent as soon as they are in the presence of the Absolute. Therefore, the Absolute must be conceptualized as independent and not confronting others on the same level. In this way, Nishida tried to understand his Absolute according to the philosophical definition of this term.

---

8. See, for example, Asami, *Dialogue*, 252.
9. See Nishida, *Last Writings*.
10. Nishida, *Last Writings*, 68–71.

Nishida's criticism of Christianity lies in that the Christian God is not conceived in the sense of the true Absolute, but in the sense of a relative. This assertion can be understood by the fact that Christianity holds the theistic view of God: God created the universe and exists outside and independent of it. In this orthodox view of the theistic conception, however, God is understood as something that exists in a confronting relationship to the world. In the traditional images of the Holy Scripture, God exists somewhere apart from the world, while sometimes intervening in it by exercising supernatural power through miracles, etc. Nishida criticizes this kind of theistic conception of the Christian God, arguing that here God is not properly conceived as the Absolute, but as a relative being who exists alongside the finite world on the same level. A typical example of this theistic relative conception of God, according to Nishida, can be found in the dialectical theology of Karl Barth. In Barthian theology (especially in its early form in *The Epistle to the Romans*), the relationship between man and God is described as a sharp confrontation in which man, the sinner, stands before God, the righteous judge. However, this understanding of God is not acceptable to Nishida, since he understands the Absolute strictly according to its philosophical definition as something that transcends all relations to other beings.

Considering this idea of the Absolute and his criticism of the Christian God, Nishida constructs his own concept of the Absolute on the basis of his theory of *place*.[11] Nishida understands place as a kind of common ground on which the confrontation and interaction of relative beings is possible. For example, in order for concrete entities such as two billiard balls to collide, there must be a billiard table or, ultimately, the law of physical causation on which the balls can interact. This billiard table or physical law is understood here as the place of two interacting balls. In the same way, in order to compare, distinguish and mix some colors such as red, blue, and green, there must be the general category of color in the field of consciousness on which these colors can be treated on the same level. Following this analogy, Nishida argues that the Absolute should not be understood as just one being among others, but as the place that encompasses all possible beings. As long as God is understood as something that confronts human beings, it is not the Absolute in the true sense.[12] Therefore, Nishida

---

11. As for Nishida's idea of place, see Nishida, "Basho."

12. In this line of thought, Nishida even argues that God the Absolute should not be understood as a being, since a being is always confronted with nonbeing. God the

characterizes his God as the Absolute that encompasses such confrontation and makes interaction and relationship possible.

This understanding of God the Absolute in Nishida has two theoretical implications that connect his theory to some current issues in contemporary philosophy of religion. First, Nishida understands his theory of the Absolute as a kind of *panentheism* (万有在神論).[13] With regard to the relationship between God and the world, panentheism recognizes itself as a middle way between Christian traditional theism and Spinozistic pantheism.[14] On the one hand, the assumption of theism, namely that a transcendent and anthropomorphic being is located outside the universe and exerts its influence on the immanent world, is hardly bearable for Nishida without theoretical modification. On the other hand, a materialistic form of pantheism is hardly a realistic option for the philosophy of religion as long as God is understood as the sum of the material world, i.e., God is reduced to a mere material being. Taking the middle way between these two positions, panentheism asserts the relationship between God and the world as such that the universe (*pan*) is *in* (*en*) God (*theos*), arguing that God is somehow immanent in the world, yet categorically transcendent and distinct from the world, holding the universe in itself. Seen in this way, it is easy to see that panentheism is an appropriate characterization of Nishida's theory of God as an absolute place. The relationship between God and the world in Nishida is understood as the world being *in* the place of God the Absolute.

Second, Nishida also characterizes his theory of the Absolute with the notion of kenosis.[15] This is related to the ontological description of God the Absolute as the place of the universe: A place is normally understood as an empty space in which an object can be located. If the place has a substantial body that occupies the space and does not allow other objects to be located, then it is no longer a place. In this sense, in order for God to become the absolute and panentheistic place that includes the universe in itself, God

---

Absolute, therefore, must be the place of "true nothing," which encompasses even the dichotomy of being and nonbeing: "The *basho* of true nothing [*shin no mu no basho*] must be that which transcends the opposition of being and nothing in every sense and enables them to be established within" (Nishida, "Basho," 57).

13. "My idea here is not pantheistic. Perhaps you will call it panentheistic" (Nishida, *Last Writings*, 70).

14. As for panentheism in general, see Clayton and Peacock, *In Whom We Live*.

15. Nishida, *Last Writings*, 70. Although the word 「ケノシス的」(kenotic) appears in the original Japanese text, the English translator put it in following way: "God must always, in St. Paul's words, empty himself."

must empty himself à la kenosis. God should not overwhelm other beings with its divinity or holiness, but should stand completely as the mere background of the universe. In this way, Nishida uses the concept of kenosis to explain the ontological status of God the Absolute.

So far, we have had a brief overview of Nishida's philosophy of religion as the background of the intercultural reception of kenosis. Starting from the strict understanding of the concept of the Absolute, which does not allow any relative counterpart, Nishida criticizes the theistic understanding of Christianity, especially the Barthian dialectical theology, in which God is seen in confrontation with man. Against this theistic *confrontation* model regarding the relationship between God and the world, Nishida proposed his panentheistic *inclusion* model using the theory of place as a metaphorical characterization of God's relationship with the universe: God is the absolute place in which the universe is included and located. And for this God-world relationship, the Absolute had to empty itself in order to make space within itself for the finite universe. Nishida used the word "kenosis" for this theoretical postulate of self-emptying. Seen in this way, Nishida's use of kenosis is almost purely theoretical, ontological, and metaphysical: as a Buddhist philosopher of religion, his theory of kenosis has nothing to do with Jesus Christ as a self-emptying figure in the original context of the Bible.

3. KITAMORI KAZOH: KENOSIS AS SOTERIOLOGY OF GOD'S EMBRACE

Kitamori's *Theology of the Pain of God* and his thought on kenosis can only be understood against the background of Nishida's philosophy of religion, which has been largely overlooked in the previous scholarship on Kitamori's theology.[16] The continuity between Kitamori and Nishida can be seen in the following two points, namely (1) the criticism of Barth's *confrontation* model and (2) the sympathy with Nishida's *inclusion* model.

First, against the prevailing trend of the rise of Barthian theology in Japanese theological discourses after World War II, Kitamori argues that Barthian theology is "unable to meet reality for us,"[17] which means that Barth's theology cannot save the people of his time. Of course, on the one hand, faced with the absolute evil of humanity as the culmination of the

16. E.g., Asami, *Dialogue*, 251–75.
17. Kitamori, *Pain of God*, 25.

First and Second World Wars, it was necessary for Barth as well as for postwar Japanese theologians to appeal to the prophetic voice that brings forth images such as the wrath of God condemning the sin of humanity. While acknowledging the necessity of this aspect of Barthian theology, Kitamori suggests that the world of his day needs more comfort than confrontation. In this regard, recognizing himself as the next generation of dialectic theology, Kitamori argues that the Barthian motif of confrontation between God and man cannot be the main principle of his own theology: "In the midst of another world tragedy after thirty years, we must imagine God differently from the way he has been recognized by the theology of the past generation."[18]

Second, as a consequence of his criticism of the Barthian *confrontation* model, Kitamori shows his sympathy for Nishida's *inclusion* model. However, this does not mean that Kitamori, as a Christian theologian, takes the position of panentheism, which would still be considered a heretical thought from the orthodox point of view. Rather, by deconstructing the ontological and metaphysical implications of Nishida's theory, Kitamori used this inclusion model for the soteriological framework of his theology:

> What is salvation? Salvation is the message that our God *enfolds* our broken reality. A God who *embraces* us completely—this is God our Savior. Is there a more astonishing miracle in the world than that God *embraces* our broken reality?[19]

Just as Nishida's panentheistic and kenotic Absolute encompasses the universe in the ontological and metaphysical sense, Kitamori's God embraces the reality of human beings broken and destroyed by sin, which should be understood in the soteriological variation of "inclusion" model. Indeed, throughout his theology of God's pain, Kitamori emphasizes that the Christian God is the God who embraces the human beings. This emphasis on the soteriological *embracing* model led to the humorous anecdote that Kitamori's theology was called "furoshiki theology" among Japanese theologians.[20] *Furoshiki* is a traditional Japanese cloth that can be used to wrap and carry various items such as books, food, or sake bottles. Against the background of Nishida's philosophy of religion, it is now clear that Kitamori adopted

---

18. Kitamori, *Pain of God*, 23.
19. Kitamori, *Pain of God*, 20; emphasis added.
20. Michalson, *Japanese Contributions to Christian Theology*, 74.

Nishida's *inclusion* model, a legacy of the Kyoto School, and developed it into an *embrace* model with a soteriological accent.

Accepting the basic principle of Nishida's inclusion theory, albeit the soteriological transformation, Kitamori now tries to respond to Nishida's criticism of the Christian God. As we have already seen, Nishida criticized Christian theism by arguing that the Christian God is not properly conceived as absolute, since God there exists as a mere relative being in opposition to the world of human beings. Kitamori's strategy for responding to this critique lies in his emphasis on economic Trinitarian theology. Although Nishida, in his critique of Christian theism, argues that God is opposed to human beings, this is only one aspect of the Trinitarian God, namely God the Father, and the role of the other two persons, namely Jesus Christ and the Holy Spirit, is not considered at all. Kitamori believes therefore that his Christian theology based on the soteriological embracing model is possible based on the reflection on the Trinitarian structure of the Christian God.[21]

The Trinitarian structure of Kitamori's theology also constitutes the core of his theology of God's pain, where his kenotic motif also becomes clear. Referring to the traditional theological notion of *ordo amoris* (the order of love), Kitamori argues that the love of God, which is at the heart of the theology, can be explained in the following three processes, in which a certain Hegelian structure can be discerned. This process consists of (1) God's love, (2) God's pain, and (3) God's love rooted in his pain.

(1) God's love: The first stage of the *ordo amoris* is God's immediate love for man. "This love of God pours immediately on its object without any hindrance."[22] Before sin entered humanity through the original sin, Adam and Eve enjoyed the immediate love of God in the garden of Eden. At that time, human beings were even the beloved children of God, just as the Christ was called the "Son" of God. However, according to Kitamori, this original and ideal relationship of God's love was lost when sin came

---

21. In fact, Kitamori's thesis submitted to Tanabe Hajime was entitled "Trinitarian Structure of the Gospel," in which his argument against Nishida's criticism of Christianity can be clearly observed ("Trinitarian Structure," 181–212.) Although this dissertation is an important piece for understanding the connection between his Kyoto School background and his theological career, it has not received enough attention in the history of research (e.g., Asami, *Dialogue*, 251–75). This dissertation shows that Kitamori's Trinitarian theology can be interpreted as his response to the legacy of the Kyoto School from his Christian theological position.

22. Kitamori, *Pain of God*, 117.

into the world. In Hegelian terms, the original and ideal state is broken by an alienation. Adam and Eve were expelled from the garden of Eden and, more importantly for Kitamori, the love of God betrayed by human beings turned into the wrath of God. "Love betrayed can only turn to anger."[23] As God's wrath then turns into God's condemnation of humanity's sin, the relationship between God and humanity can be characterized as *confrontation* as in Barth's theology. Kitamori therefore argues that the Barthian model of "confrontation" is placed as the first stage of the whole process of the *ordo amoris*. However, it is only the first of the three levels of the whole process, and only one part of the whole Trinitarian structure. It is therefore at the same time Kitamori's answer to Nishida's criticism of Christianity that the Barthian confrontation model does not exhaust the whole God-world relationship in Christianity.

(2) God's pain: In the second process of *God's pain*, all the key concepts of Kitamori's theology come into play, namely, the Trinitarian structure, the kenotic motif, the *embrace* model, etc. The paradox of the Christian gospel lies in the fact that God did not condemn those who deserved it, but embraced them: "God did not repulse those who should be repulsed; he enfolded and embraced them."[24] This pain of God, through which the wrath of God, the alienation of the first level, is overcome, is brought by Jesus Christ, the Second Person of the Trinity, and his kenotic death on the cross. As in the biblical narrative of the kenosis, although Christ existed "in the form of God," he "did not regard equality with God," "emptied himself" and "humbled himself," took the "form of slaves," "became obedient to the point of death," "even death on the cross" (Phil 2:6–8).[25] In order to save humanity in this confrontation, God sent his only Son to die on the cross, as in the traditional Christian narrative of salvation. Through this pain of God, the pain of a parent who loses his only child,[26] God overcame the relationship of confrontation and began the relationship of embrace. Although this soteriological *embrace* is something different from the ontological *inclusion* in Nishida's philosophy of religion, the category of *God's pain* is in this sense the core of Kitamori's response to Nishida's critique of Christianity:

23. Kitamori, *Pain of God*, 118.

24. Kitamori, *Pain of God*, 119.

25. Scripture quotations in this chapter are from the NRSVue.

26. Avoiding the criticism of Patripassianism, a form of heresy, Kitamori argues that the Trinitarian understanding of God's pain is not a substantial, but a relational concept. (*Pain of God*, 16).

the Christian Trinitarian God is not only God the Father who confronts us as in Barthian theology, but also the God who embraces us through the pain of losing Jesus Christ the Son.

(3) Finally, the *ordo amoris* culminates in the third and highest level, "God's love rooted in his pain."[27] In Kitamori's words, "The victory of his pain is in fact love rooted in the pain of God."[28] The first level of God's wrath as alienation is overcome by the second level of God's pain, and thus the third level of "God's love rooted in his pain" is established as the restoration of God's original love. Although this is the culmination and highest attainment of God's love, Kitamori sees the decisive point of the *ordo amoris* in the second level of God's pain, as the initiative of God's love is manifested in this middle point of the whole process: "the three orders of love are seen inclusively in the one order—the 'pain of God.'"[29] God's pain is, as the title of his book suggests, the central principle of Kitamori's theology.

In sum, Kitamori's kenotic conception in his theology of God's pain can be understood as his response to his Kyoto School background, or more precisely, to Nishida's critique of Christianity. While Nishida criticized the Christian theistic God who confronts human beings and thus is not properly conceived as the Absolute, Kitamori argued that this God of confrontation, or in his own words, God's wrath, should be placed in the whole picture of the Trinitarian structure. The God of confrontation is overcome by the kenotic motif of God's pain, which embraces alienated human beings and welcomes them into the restored love of God rooted in God's pain. Although this soteriological embrace is conceived differently from Nishida's ontological and metaphysical model of inclusion, this is

---

27. Since the first order of God's love/wrath and the second order of God's pain each correspond to the persons of the Father and the Son in the Trinitarian structure, it is naturally expected that the third order of "God's love rooted in his pain" also corresponds to the Holy Spirit. However, in his account of the *ordo amoris*, Kitamori somehow does not give much consideration to the role of the Holy Spirit. Despite his emphasis on the Trinitarian structure, the role of the Holy Spirit is relatively ignored throughout Kitamori's theology of God's pain. In this regard, it is necessary to note that Mutō Kazuo (武藤一雄), also a Christian philosopher of religion who originated from the Kyoto School, placed more emphasis on the role of the Holy Spirit in his "Theological Philosophy of Religion." The contrast between Kitamori and Mutō will be an important moment to consider the relationship between the Kyoto School and Christianity. See Mutō, *Christianity and Notion of Nothingness*. Also for the tradition of Christian studies in the Kyoto School, see Repp, "Buddhist-Christian Dialogue."

28. Kitamori, *Pain of God*, 121.

29. Kitamori, *Pain of God*, 122.

how Kitamori attempted to take up Nishida's philosophy of religion and his critique of Christianity. As Kitamori comments: "The pain of God is an all-embracing principle."[30]

4. JÜRGEN MOLTMANN: KENOSIS AS THE PRINCIPLE OF SOLIDARITY AND LIBERATION

As already seen in the introduction, Kitamori's kenotic theology of God's pain flows into Moltmann's political theology, which today is recognized as one of the most important sources of kenotic theory in modern Christian theology. Although Kitamori and Moltmann can be compared in many respects (for example, the emphasis on the theology of the cross as opposed to the theology of glory,[31] or the Trinitarian understanding of kenosis,[32] etc.), this study will only briefly point out that Moltmann elaborated the motif of kenosis and Kitamori's idea of God's pain into the ethico-political category of solidarity.

> Christian theology finds its identity as such in the cross of Christ. . . . The crucified Christ became the brother of the despised, abandoned and oppressed. And this is why brotherhood with the "least of his brethren" is a necessary part of brotherhood with Christ and identification with him. Thus Christian theology must be worked out amongst these people and with them. . . . Christian identification with the crucified Christ means solidarity with the

---

30. Kitamori, *Pain of God*, 144. The main argument of this study, namely that Kitamori's theology should be interpreted against the background of the Kyoto School, can also be confirmed by the following quote from his thesis: "God the Absolute is never limited in His Absoluteness by the existence of the relative world outside of Him. God the Absolute truly demonstrates His Absoluteness by embracing the world of the relative within His own love. The Absolute that stands in opposition to the relative is never the true Absolute. For it ceases to be absolute when it opposes the relative. The true Absolute is not the Absolute that merely opposes the relative, but the Absolute that embraces the relative in its own love" ("Trinitarian Structure," 198).

31. Moltmann, *Crucified God*, 207.

32. See, for example, Moltmann's remark on the cross of Christ: "If the kenosis of the Son to the point of death upon the cross is the 'revelation of the entire Trinity,' this event too can only be presented as a God-event in trinitarian terms. . . . The cross stands at the heart of the trinitarian being of God; it divides and conjoins the persons in their relationships to each other and portrays them in a specific way. For as we said, the theological dimension of the death of Jesus on the cross is what happens between Jesus and his Father in the spirit of abandonment and surrender" (*Crucified God*, 206–7.)

sufferings of the poor and the misery both of the oppressed and the oppressors.[33]

The identity of Christian theology is nothing but the cross of Christ, and Christ became the brother of the oppressed through his pain of the cross. Therefore, the task of Christian theology is also to go out into the streets and show solidarity with these brothers. In this way, Moltmann tries to transform the idea of Christ's pain into an ethical and political category.

Moltmann continues to argue as follows:

> Christian theology must be theology of the cross, if it is to be identified as Christian theology through Christ. But the theology of the cross is a critical and liberating theory of God and man. Christian life is a form of practice which consists in following the crucified Christ, and it changes both man himself and the circumstances in which he lives. To this extent, a theology of the cross is a practical theory.[34]

The identity of Christian theology is nothing other than the cross of Christ, and the cross of Christ is for Moltmann nothing other than the symbol of solidarity and liberation. Therefore, Christian theology must also function as a means for the liberation of the oppressed and despised. In this way, Moltmann linked the cross of Christ and Kitamori's category of pain to his agenda of political theology, in which compassion, solidarity, and liberation are envisaged.

5. CONCLUSION: TYPOLOGIES OF KENOTIC THOUGHTS AND PROSPECTS

This study attempted to describe the intercultural intellectual history of the kenosis between Japanese and German theology in the light of the method of global intellectual history. Nishida Kitaro, the Japanese philosopher of the Kyoto School, began with his theory of the Absolute, which is to be conceived in the *inclusion* model against the Barthian *confrontation* model. Nishida thus developed a philosophy of religion based on his theory of place, in which God the Absolute is seen as the panentheistic and kenotic place of nothingness in which the whole universe is located. Following this *inclusion* model, Kazoh Kitamori, a Christian theologian, elaborated

---

33. Moltmann, *Crucified God*, 24–25.
34. Moltmann, *Crucified God*, 25.

his theology of God's pain in the line of Trinitarian kenosis. The Barthian *confrontation* model, namely God and his wrath confronting human sin, does not exhaust the Christian doctrine of God, but it is only one moment of the whole Trinitarian structure. The crux of the gospel lies in the pain of Christ on the cross, which overcomes the alienation of God's wrath and brings human beings into the embrace of the Trinitarian God, which can be understood as the Christian soteriological variation of Nishida's *inclusion* model. This line of intellectual history in the Kyoto School was finally taken up by the German theologian Jürgen Moltmann, who integrated Kitamori's theology of pain into a practical and political category. Reflection on the kenosis of Christ and his death on the cross necessarily leads to solidarity and liberation of the oppressed. So far, the main task of this study, namely to exemplify the global historical description of the intellectual history of kenosis, has been fulfilled, at least to a certain extent.

As a perspective for further discussion, I would like to propose a typology of kenotic thought that would be helpful in articulating and understanding the various intercultural and interreligious discussions in this volume. In reviewing the various forms of kenotic thought, whether or not they are addressed in this chapter or in this volume, one could observe at least two fundamentally different aspects of kenosis; one is what one might call the *ethical-practical aspect* of kenosis, and the other is its *ontological-metaphysical aspect*.

The ethical-practical aspect of kenosis emphasizes, on the one hand, that the kenotic motif of self-sacrifice leads to the ethical-practical requirement of service to others. This aspect derives directly from the original context of kenosis in Paul's theology in the Letter to the Philippians; the kenosis of Christ, who emptied himself and humbled himself to take human form to die on the cross, was the normative example of Paul's altruistic ethics: "Do nothing from selfish ambition or empty conceit, but in humility regard others as better than yourselves" (Phil 2:3). The development of this ethical-practical aspect is typically seen in Francis of Assisi, who renounced his wealthy family background and lived in honorable poverty. It is no coincidence that the symbolic reference to this kenotic saint can be found not only in the Christian church today, which is in urgent need of internal reform (see Pope Francis in the Catholic Church), but also in the Buddhist kenotic philosopher, as in Nishitani Keiji.[35]

---

35. Nishitani, *Religion and Nothingness*, 280.

This ethical-practical aspect of kenosis was then developed to emphasize its political implication in the recent phenomenon of the so-called political turn. While the traditional form of kenotic ethics tended to remain in the relatively narrow, interpersonal realm of charity, this new development brought into play a new dimension, namely the need for collective and political solidarity in order to serve the oppressed and actively fight against social injustice. Here the image of kenosis as self-humiliation and self-sacrifice is used to symbolize solidarity with the oppressed in sociopolitical reality. As already analyzed (albeit partially) in this chapter, this political development of kenosis is represented by Jürgen Moltmann.

In addition to this ethical-practical aspect, it can be said that there is another fundamentally different strand of kenotic thought which can be characterized as its ontological-metaphysical aspect. Here, the idea of kenosis is understood as an ontological and metaphysical principle of fundamental reality and worldview. For example, as explained in this essay, Nishida Kitaro used the idea of kenosis to characterize his Absolute as the panentheistic unity between God and the world. In order for the absoluteness of the Absolute to be taken seriously, Nishida argued that the Absolute must be understood as the place of absolute nothingness that negates or empties itself to become the place for the finite world. This association of kenosis with absolute nothingness and the Mahāyāna Buddhist idea of emptiness can be seen as the Kyoto School's contribution to the history of the concept of kenosis as it can be seen in the tradition from Nishida, Nishitani up to Abe Masao.

Summarized in this way, it might seem that there is a clear boundary of kenotic thought between Buddhism and Christianity. But this is, of course, an oversimplification. Although such a tendency certainly exists, these two aspects of kenotic thought are more or less shared by both religious traditions. On the one hand, some Christian theologians are pursuing the theoretical possibility of introducing the ontological-metaphysical aspect of kenosis into the doctrine of God through their dialogue with other religious traditions. The Absolute in the strict sense of emptiness is certainly only conceivable in Mahāyāna Buddhism, but some Christian theologians try to incorporate the idea of a kenotic Absolute in the form of a panentheism,[36] which at least has the resonance of Nishida's conception of

---

36. As for panentheism, see Clayton and Peacock, *In Whom We Live*. Regarding the dialogue between panentheism and world religions, see Biernacki and Clayton, *Panentheism Across World's Traditions*.

the Absolute. Although there would be problems and criticisms regarding the Christian conception of God in terms of panentheism, this attempt is worth mentioning as a Christian approach to the ontological-metaphysical aspect of kenosis.[37]

On the other hand, the ethical-practical aspect of kenosis is by no means neglected in Buddhism. A notable example is Nishitani Keiji's kenotic account of ethics and charity from the perspective of Mahāyāna emptiness in his seminal work *Religion and Nothingness*.[38] In this respect, Nishitani's philosophy of religion is an exemplary theorization of Buddhist kenotic thought in that it builds a bridge between the ontological-metaphysical aspect as the principle of emptiness and its ethical-practical concretization in the ethics of selfless love.[39] The dialogue between Buddhism and Christianity on the idea of kenosis is, in this regard, already characterized by mutual learning and mutual transformation, which is one of the most ideal virtues of interreligious dialogue.[40]

Let us conclude this typological summary by inviting both traditions to further reflection. On the one hand, it would be worthwhile for Christianity to revisit the dialogue with Mahāyāna Buddhism represented by the Kyoto School, whose scholarship is undergoing a fundamental transformation. Although the Buddhism-Christianity dialogue flourished in the second half of the twentieth century, Buddhism is of course not considered today as a partner in urgent dialogue compared to Islam or the Eastern Orthodox Church. However, the Kyoto School is not the same as it was in the twentieth century, at least in two respects. First, the subject matter has diversified; whereas in the past the Kyoto School's studies focused mainly on Mahāyāna Buddhist theory, today it is expanding to include topics such as technology, post-colonialism, or cognitive science. Second, researchers have also diversified; whereas Kyoto School scholarship used to be represented by the homogeneous group of Japanese Buddhists, it is now carried out in different countries and cultures in the context of world philosophy. In view of this recent development, it is worthwhile for Christianity to

---

37. In addition to panentheism, the kabbalistic "zimzum" could also be seen as the ontological-metaphysical motif of kenosis in the Judeo-Christian tradition. For example, see Jonas, *Gottesbegriff nach Auschwitz*, 45; Moltmann, *Gott in der Schöpfung*, 98.

38. Nishitani, *Religion and Nothingness*, esp. ch. 6, "Śūnyatā and History," 218–85.

39. On Nishitani and Kenosis, see Miriam-Sonja Hantke's contribution in this volume and the following studies: Odin, "'Kenōsis' as Foundation for Dialogue"; Bartneck, "Kenosis."

40. Cobb, *Beyond Dialogue*.

revisit the legacy of the Kyoto School, especially in its confrontation with the still prevailing Eurocentrism.

On the other hand, the challenge for the Buddhist Kyoto School can be summarized in the following concrete question: Is the political theory based on the Mahāyāna Buddhist kenosis possible? In general, it can be said that the sociopolitical dimension was not the main concern of Buddhism, at least in terms of its origin as a secluded religion. Nishida already pointed out that Buddhism "did not avoid being other-worldly."[41] This point can also be seen in Nishitani's kenotic ethics. Although, as already mentioned, it is an exemplary formulation of Buddhist ethics on the basis of kenotic emptiness, in my opinion it still remains in the interpersonal realm and lacks the political dimension that would make possible the active and systematic confrontation with social injustice. Of course, the current trend of so-called engaged Buddhism would be one of the possible answers to this problem. In our context, however, it is certainly worth asking whether the scholarship of the Kyoto School can theoretically contribute to the formation of Buddhist political theory. In this regard, the growing research on the social ontology of the Kyoto School could be a key to this task.[42] The dialogue between Buddhism and Christianity continues in the twenty-first century with different themes and concepts.

BIBLIOGRAPHY

Asami, Yō. *Dialogue Between Nishida Kitaro and Christianity*. Tokyo: Chōbunsha, 2000.
Bartneck, Tobias. "Kenosis Seen from the Standpoint of Nishitani Keiji: Towards a New Understanding of the Kyoto School's Interpretation of Christianity." *Kyushin* 28 (2023) 199–213.
Bayly, Christopher A. *The Birth of the Modern World, 1780–1914: Global Connections and Comparisons*. Oxford: Blackwell, 2004.
Biernacki, Loriliai, and Philip Clayton, eds. *Panentheism Across the World's Traditions*. Oxford: Oxford University, 2014.
Brück, Michael von, and Whalen Lai. *Buddhismus und Christentum: Geschichte, Konfrontation, Dialog*. Munich: Beck, 1997.
Clayton, Philip, and Arthur Peacocke, eds. *In Whom We Live and Move and Have Our Being: Panentheistic Reflections on God's Presence in a Scientific World*. Grand Rapids: Eerdmans, 2004.

41. "Now the Buddhism that took its rise in Indian soil was very profound as religious truth, but it did not avoid being other-worldly. Even Mahayana Buddhism did not truly attain to the world-creatively real in the sense I have just indicated" (Nishida, *Last Writings*, 102).

42. As for the social ontology of the Kyoto School, see Urai, *Tanabe Hajime*.

PART II. KENOSIS IN THE KYOTO SCHOOL

Cobb, John B., Jr. *Beyond Dialogue: Toward a Mutual Transformation of Christianity and Buddhism*. Philadelphia: Fortress, 1982.

Conrad, Sebastian. *What Is Global History?* Princeton, NJ: Princeton University Press, 2016.

Jonas, Hans. *Der Gottesbegriff nach Auschwitz: Eine jüdische Stimme*. Frankfurt am Main: Suhrkamp, 1987.

Kitamori, Kazoh. "In Memory of Prof. Tanabe." *Journal of Philosophical Studies* 42 (1964) 676–77.

———. *Theology of the Pain of God*. Richmond, VA: John Knox, 1965.

———. "Trinitarian Structure of the Gospel." *Journal of Philosophical Studies* 27 (1994) 181–212.

Michalson, Carl. *Japanese Contributions to Christian Theology*. Philadelphia: Westminster, 1965.

Moltmann, Jürgen. *The Crucified God: The Cross of Christ as the Foundation and Criticism of Christian Theology*. Minneapolis: Fortress, 1993.

———. *Gott in der Schöpfung: Ökologische Schöpfungslehre*. Munich: Kaiser, 1985.

Morimoto, Anri. "Editor's Preface: Re-Questioning the 'Japanese Theology.'" *Theology in Japan* 52 (2013) 1–4.

Moyn, Samuel, and Andrew Sartori, eds. *Global Intellectual History*. New York: Columbia University Press, 2013.

Mutō, Kazuo. *Christianity and the Notion of Nothingness: Contribution to Buddhist-Christian Dialogue from the Kyoto School*. Edited by Martin Repp. Translated by Jan van Bragt. Philosophy of Religion: World Religions 2. Boston: Brill, 2012.

Nishida, Kitarō. "Basho." In *Place and Dialectic: Two Essays by Nishida Kitaro*, translated by John W. M. Krummel and Shigenori Nagatomo, 49–102. New York: Oxford University Press, 2012.

———. *Last Writings: Nothingness and the Religious Worldview*. Translated by David A. Dilworth. Honolulu: University of Hawaii Press, 1987.

Nishitani, Keiji. *Religion and Nothingness*. Translated by Jan van Bragt. Nanzan Studies in Religion and Culture. Berkeley: University of California Press, 1982.

Odin, Steve. "'Kenōsis' as a Foundation for Buddhist-Christian Dialogue: The Kenotic Buddhology of Nishida and Nishitani of the Kyoto School in Relation to the Kenotic Christology of Thomas J. J. Altizer." *Eastern Buddhist* 1 (1987) 34–61.

Repp, Martin. "Buddhist-Christian Dialogue and the Kyoto School." In *The Routledge Handbook of Buddhist-Christian Studies*, edited by Carol S. Anderson and Thomas Cattoi. Routledge Handbooks in Religion. London: Routledge, 2023.

Takeda, Atsushi. *The Story of the "Kyoto School": Friendships and Conflicts Among Intellectuals*. Tokyo: Chuōkōronshinsha, 2012.

Urai, Satoshi. *Tanabe Hajime: The Philosophy of Social Reality and Salvation*. Kyoto: Kyoto University Press, 2024.

6

The Kenosis of the Rational

Tanabe Hajime's Philosophical Failure and the Violent Implications of Human Rationality

SATOSHI URAI

INTRODUCTION: IS THE RATIONAL ALWAYS BETTER THAN THE IRRATIONAL?

"Is being rational inherently good?" "Is being moral inherently good?"—Across cultures and eras, those who answer no to these questions are undoubtedly in the minority. This chapter aims to provide a perspective for rethinking these questions that most people naturally affirm. Of course, our purpose is *not* to exalt the value of the irrational or the immoral; rather, we seek to demonstrate that the rational and the moral possess violence no less than that of the irrational and the immoral.

To achieve this, the chapter examines the philosophical failures and subsequent reconstruction of the philosophy of Tanabe Hajime (田辺元, 1885–1962), one of modern Japan's foremost philosophers and a cofounder of the Kyoto School, which has gained international recognition in recent years. What emerges from this investigation is the violent and exclusionary nature of human rational thought. It is precisely for this reason that philosophy, in its pursuit of truth, must be a form of reflection not merely *about* the Absolute but *with* the Absolute. This suggests a philosophy necessitating the kenosis of the Absolute—a philosophy of religion in which knowledge is "mediated by the self-negating kenosis of the Absolute's love."[1] In other words, until 1941, Tanabe explored the pursuit of absolute knowledge through the process of becoming increasingly rational. However, by 1944, he had abandoned this approach, instead arguing that absolute knowledge can be attained only through the kenosis of the Absolute, or the absolutely rational. The latter is the philosophical stance Tanabe arrived at through his failures and fundamental turn.

Let us begin by clarifying the relationship between this chapter's central problem and Tanabe's philosophy. Rationality is generally considered a virtue in society. In contemporary times, morality, too, is often regarded as an indispensable requirement for societal membership. Yet, to demand that everyone always act morally without fail is unrealistic. Of course, those who ordinarily act morally would not be harshly condemned even if they occasionally faltered. What becomes critical when society passes judgment on a transgressor is whether they acted with "right" motives. Consequently, we should strive to improve society and our neighbors based on "right" motives. Still, how does this notion sound to *you*, the reader? If you find this reasoning compelling, the label for your position in the near future might be exclusionism—or perhaps totalitarianism. The latter is the path Tanabe, *much to his own dismay*, ended up treading in 1939.

Of course, Tanabe was not—contrary to how his philosophy is often misunderstood—building a philosophy to justify totalitarianism from the outset. On the contrary, amid the rise of totalitarianism during Japan's Fifteen-Year War (1931–45), he sought to make Japan a more rational and moral state, developing a theory he believed could achieve this.[2] This theory, developed between 1934 and 1941, was the social ontology known as the "logic of species" (種の論理). Its development halted in 1941 because Tanabe, who initially aimed to critique totalitarianism, found himself complicit in it. Saying this might make Tanabe appear to be a naïve philosopher who failed to construct his theory. Yet his failure exposed the inherent violence within rational and moral perspectives—not only are they constantly at risk of becoming exclusionism, but they are also linked to totalitarianism.

The link between rationality or morality and exclusionism or totalitarianism might seem counterintuitive. Yet, Tanabe's philosophical trajectory

1. THZ 10:53.
2. THZ 6:399; THZ 7:253.

demonstrated precisely this: an attempt to rationalize society can lead to totalitarianism. Tanabe himself was a man of exceptional moral rigor, a fact underscored by his longtime colleague Takahashi Satomi (高橋里美, 1886–1964), who remarked, "He clad himself in the impenetrable armor of moral ought."[3] Reflecting this disposition, Tanabe's philosophy was imbued with a longing for the "better," and his desire to improve society persisted throughout his career.

Until 1941, this yearning appeared as a profound aspiration for rationality and morality underpinning his philosophy. For example, Tanabe identified one reason for constructing the logic of species as anguish "at the strength of self-attachment," including his own.[4] This motivation is hardly incomprehensible—it resonates with the frustrations we often feel toward those who are in positions of responsibility today, such as politicians, bureaucrats, and business leaders. Thus, the aspiration to build a better society alongside those who act for others and society with "right" motives aligns entirely with the practical impetus of Tanabe's logic of species.

If this is the case, why did Tanabe's philosophy, grounded in such seemingly "upright" aspirations, end up reinforcing totalitarianism? The answer lies in his unwavering trust in rationality. This belief holds that implementing rationality necessarily leads to a more rational and thus better society.

In the following sections, we elucidate the violent implications of this belief, demonstrating the limits and collapse of human rational thought that Tanabe called the "inescapable fate of reason."[5] This will highlight the significance of a philosophy necessitating kenosis—a turn from a philosophy *of* the absolute to a philosophy *with* the Absolute. To achieve this, the chapter is organized as follows: Section 1 outlines the development of Tanabe's philosophy in this chapter's context. Section 2 explores the concept of "self-conscious purposiveness" (自覚的合目的性) to clarify what Tanabe meant by "rationality." Section 3 reveals the "inescapable fate of reason" inherent in self-conscious purposiveness, connecting it with Tanabe's pivotal notion of the "antinomies of practical reason." Section 4 discusses the philosophical turn Tanabe underwent in confronting reason's fate, thereby elucidating the significance of a philosophy necessitating kenosis.

---

3. Takahashi, *Complete Works*, 207.
4. THZ 6:451.
5. THZ 9:52.

PART II. KENOSIS IN THE KYOTO SCHOOL

1. TANABE HAJIME: A PHILOSOPHER CONFRONTING THE LIMITS OF HUMAN REASON

This section aims to provide an overview of the philosophical development of Tanabe. While there are some comprehensive introductions to Tanabe's thought,[6] we revisit his philosophy in light of its specific context within this chapter, especially given his limited exposure internationally due to the scarcity of translations, despite being a prominent figure in modern Japanese philosophy.

Tanabe began his philosophical career with "On Thetic Judgment" (1910), which is regarded as a revised version of his bachelor thesis. From then until 1926, including his European studies mainly in Berlin and Freiburg (1922–24), he sought to synthesize neo-Kantianism, phenomenology, and the philosophy of Nishida Kitarō[7] (西田幾多郎, 1870–1945) into a single framework that he called "the metaphysics of the I" (我の形而上学)[8] or "the metaphysics of the subject" (主観の形而上学).[9] This attempt stopped in his first unfinished manuscript, "Intuitive Understanding and the Thing-in-Itself" (1925–26). Following this unfinished work, Tanabe began to investigate the logic of dialectic, concerned that "the materialist dialectic, which was rapidly gaining influence among university students at the time, was regarded by some uncritical adherents as an omnipotent logic—a kind of magic wand capable of instantaneously acquiring all scientific knowledge."[10] However, since "at the time, my [Tanabe's] thinking was predominantly shaped by the logical framework of the Marburg School's neo-Kantianism,"[11] this study attempted to observe dialectic from the outside, and he realized that this attempt did not have the ability to understand it precisely in the first place. Consequently, "The Logic of Dialectic" (1927–29), which developed this attempt, became Tanabe's second unfinished work. Since half of Tanabe's unfinished works, of which there were only four in his lifetime, are concentrated in the period 1925–29, we can see the philosophical anguish that Tanabe experienced during this time.

---

6. Heisig, *Philosophers of Nothingness*; Morisato, *Tanabe Hajime and Kyoto School*; Urai, "Shinran's Concept of *Jinen Honi*."

7. Nishida, alongside Tanabe, laid the foundation of the Kyoto School and remains its central figure.

8. THZ 2:167.

9. THZ 1:452.

10. THZ 3:77.

11. THZ 3:77.

Thereafter, Tanabe abandoned the neo-Kantian foundation of his thought and began constructing his own dialectical standpoint, which he called "absolute dialectic" (he labeled this with the German word *Sachlichkeitsdialektik*). As Sugimura demonstrated, this standpoint sought to synthesize dialectic (Hegel and Marx), phenomenology (Husserl and Heidegger), and Nishida philosophy into one cohesive system. Tanabe's stay in Freiburg was instrumental in shaping this development. He learned from Heidegger that phenomenology's imperative "to the things themselves!" (*zu den Sachen selbst!*) signified not a static orientation but a dynamic mobility (*Bewegtheit*).[12]

Yet by 1929, he realized that dialectic—not the transcendental philosophy he had previously associated with neo-Kantianism and phenomenology—was the appropriate method for capturing this mobility. Tanabe's absolute dialectic, as expressed in *Sachlichkeitsdialektik*, sought to fulfill phenomenology's imperative more effectively by integrating its insights within a dialectical framework. The designation of "absolute nothingness" for the principle of mediation and sublation—the "principle of dialectic"[13]— central to his dialectic clearly reflects the influence of Nishida's concept of absolute nothingness. After the absolute dialectic is established, it is then developed into a social ontology, the logic of species that aims to make society rational by properly grasping the mobility of historical society.

Behind Tanabe's intellectual trajectory—the metaphysics of the I, absolute dialectic, and the logic of species—was what he described, borrowing Hegel's conception in *Lectures on the Philosophy of History*, as "trust in reason."[14] This attitude of Tanabe is most directly and frankly expressed in the following passage from his lecture:

> Hegel's notion that "what is rational is actual" is neither mere rationalism nor optimism. For us to live, it is necessary to believe that actuality is rational, even if it is not rational today, it is something that can be rationalized, and in essence it is rational. I think we cannot live even a single day without the conviction that justice will ultimately triumph. I believe that this conviction is the conviction that sustains our life.[15]

---

12. Sugimura, "Phenomenology Touching Its Limits," 118.
13. THZ 6:441.
14. THZ 3:182.
15. THZ 15:230.

Here, Tanabe interprets Hegel's famous proposition in *Elements of the Philosophy of Right* that "what is rational is actual; and what is actual is rational."[16] His interpretation is as follows. While the current actuality in front of us often appears irrational and immoral, such a perception would lead us to despair. To avoid this, Tanabe claimed, we must believe that actuality is essentially rational, that actuality is moving in a rational direction, and that justice will prevail in the end. This is what Tanabe calls "trust in reason," and it is later conceptualized as "faith in the absolute good" during the period of the logic of species.[17]

As expressed in *Hegelian Philosophy and Dialectic* (1932), where Tanabe constructs his absolute dialectic, stating that "philosophy's absolute knowledge is found in the self-consciousness of praxis,"[18] the absolute knowledge in Tanabe's dialectic is realized within society through individual praxis—praxis endowed with "self-conscious purposiveness," which will be discussed in the next section. In other words, the ideal of the human being presented in Tanabe's philosophy of the 1930s consists in individuals who believe that the world can improve through their own hands and who persist in moral praxis. Supporting this praxis, absolute nothingness is positioned not only as the principle governing mediation and sublation but also as the "principle of morality."[19] That is, absolute nothingness, through mediation and sublation, imparts morality to human beings. For this reason, Tanabe's absolute knowledge is intrinsically moral. Because of this moral character of absolute knowledge as praxis, individuals who attain absolute knowledge can make society "better," that is, more moral and rational. In this manner, Hegel's dictum that "what is rational is actual; and what is actual is rational" emerges as a central tenet of the logic of species, representing the ideal that individuals ought to realize in actuality.[20]

However, the logic of species, constructed from 1934 with the aim of rationalizing society through individual praxis, reached a troubling conclusion by 1939, the year World War II began, asserting that "obedience to the commands of the state" constituted the realization of human freedom.[21] This totalitarian outcome, however, arose not as an aberration but as a

---

16. Hegel, *Philosophy of Right*, 20.
17. THZ 6:223.
18. THZ 3:81.
19. THZ 3:511.
20. THZ 6:507.
21. THZ 7:41.

logical consequence of Tanabe's vision to rationalize and moralize society under the extreme situation of war. It was precisely this result that led Tanabe, after the war, to renounce his earlier philosophy based on his *trust in reason* and to advocate instead philosophy as metanoetics, centered on the "*powerlessness of reason*"[22] and a shift from a "philosophy of self-power" to a "philosophy of Other-power."[23]

This radical turn—from a philosophy of the absolute grounded in trust in reason to a philosophy with the Absolute rooted in its kenosis—will be gradually examined in the following sections. Next, we turn to the concept of "self-conscious purposiveness," which Tanabe found in Kant's *Critique of Judgement* and which defines the "goodness" at the heart of Tanabe's vision for improving society.

2. SELF-CONSCIOUS PURPOSIVENESS AS ABSOLUTE KNOWLEDGE

Let us begin by clarifying the term "self-consciousness" (自覚) within the context of self-conscious purposiveness. In the Kyoto School, self-consciousness holds a special significance. It is undeniably a key concept in Nishida's philosophy, and many Kyoto School philosophers influenced by him also placed great importance on it. However, the term itself was widely used in modern Japan and was not invented by Nishida.

That said, starting with *Intuition and Reflection in Self-Consciousness* (1917), Nishida imparted his own distinctive meaning to it. Nishida's unique definition of self-consciousness can be succinctly summarized as "the self seeing itself."[24] Nishida deepened his thought by reflecting on the "seeing self," the "seen self," and the act of "seeing." As evidenced by his well-known 1943 essay "On Self-Consciousness," written two years before his death, self-consciousness remained central to his philosophical inquiry throughout his life.

In contrast, self-consciousness did not play the same central role in Tanabe's philosophy. While his early work was undoubtedly influenced by Nishida—especially *An Inquiry into the Good* (1911) and *Intuition and Reflection*—he explicitly employed the term "self-consciousness" as a key concept only in *Kant's Teleology* (1924), a work written under Nishida's

---

22. THZ 14:423; emphasis added.
23. THZ 9:236.
24. NKZ 12:67.

influence. This is not to say that the term disappears from his later works; in fact, it appears frequently. However, Tanabe describes it as a "term peculiar to dialectic" and defines it as the state of becoming "für sich" in recognizing something.[25] In other words, for Tanabe, self-consciousness was simply one of the basic tools of his philosophy, rather than a central concept as it was for Nishida. For Tanabe, self-consciousness refers to "knowledge or cognition that has reached the for-itself stage." For instance, an adult can affirm their identity as a human being—something an infant cannot do. This kind of recognition is what Tanabe means by self-consciousness.[26] In this sense, self-conscious purposiveness can be understood as "purposiveness recognized at the for-itself stage."

What, then, is purposiveness? To clarify this, we first examine the background of *Kant's Teleology*. As noted in the previous section, Tanabe stayed in Europe from 1922 to 1924, primarily to study under Husserl. Reflecting on this experience, he recalled how his exposure to German philosophers influenced his writing of *Kant's Teleology* in its preface to the reprint edition (1948):

> The primary motivation was that I came to realize the limitations of the *Philosophie der Wissenschaft* while studying under Husserl. As a positive aspect to this negative aspect, I resonated with the demands for a worldview philosophy, which had gained prominence in German philosophical circles after World War I. Upon returning to Japan in 1924, coinciding with the bicentennial of Kant's birth, I was tasked with giving a commemorative lecture. This occasion led me to make Kant's teleology the focus of my first academic undertaking.[27]

During his time with Husserl, Tanabe became aware of the limitations inherent in his standpoint, mainly based on the "philosophy of science" (*Philosophie der Wissenschaft*),[28] which he associates with thinkers such as Cohen, Windelband, Rickert, and Cassirer. In response, he turned to the

---

25. THZ 3:244.

26. Thus, this chapter does not translate it as "self-awareness," as is often done to give it a special meaning.

27. THZ 3:8.

28. The *Philosophie der Wissenschaft* stands in contrast to the philosophy of life (*Philosophie des Lebens*) advanced by figures such as Dilthey, Simmel, and Bergson (THZ 4:37–38). Tanabe described the former as follows: "In short, a philosophy that takes scientific cognition as its object while demanding itself to be a form of scientific cognition is what we refer to as the 'philosophy of science'" (THZ 4:37).

challenge of constructing a worldview philosophy. As a means of pursuing this, he chose to focus on Kant's teleology, particularly the moral teleology presented in the latter part of *The Critique of Judgment*.

To connect this to the "trust in reason" discussed in the previous section, the moral teleology that Tanabe discovered in Kant provided Tanabe with a sense of purposiveness—an orientation toward a rational society. To "self-consciously" recognize this orientation is what Tanabe meant by self-conscious purposiveness.

Tanabe defines self-conscious purposiveness in *Kant's Teleology* as "becoming self-conscious of purposiveness for oneself in something outside of oneself, which is independent of oneself."[29] In other words, self-conscious purposiveness refers to recognizing the purposive direction given to oneself within the whole world and actualizing that direction through one's own decisions.

In *Kant's Teleology*, self-conscious purposiveness is presented as the synthesis of the "dialectic of will."[30] The dialectic of will is Tanabe's interpretation of the concepts of purposiveness expounded by Kant in *The Critique of Judgment*, restructured within a dialectical framework. According to Tanabe, Kant discussed three kinds of purposiveness here:

1. Formal purposiveness
2. Inner purposiveness
3. Self-conscious purposiveness (a term introduced by Tanabe, though Kant himself did not name it)

Tanabe saw formal purposiveness and inner purposiveness as the thesis and antithesis in the dialectic of will, while self-conscious purposiveness served as the synthesis. Tanabe explains formal purposiveness as "the notion that nature, by virtue of the immanence of ideals, is organized in a way that it is comprehensible to our cognitive faculties"[31] and inner purposiveness as the idea that "natural entities form what is called a natural purpose (*Naturzweck*), in which the whole is the result and the cause simultaneously, as each part mutually depends on each other to form the whole, and at the same time, the concept of the whole also conditions the form

---

29. THZ 3:64.
30. THZ 3:4.
31. THZ 3:14.

and combination of each part."³² In simpler terms, formal purposiveness refers to the purposiveness that we find in nature, while inner purposiveness pertains to the purposiveness inherent within nature itself as an object. As the synthesis of these two, self-conscious purposiveness unifies subject and object, allowing "the subject, from the standpoint of free will, to imbue deterministic nature with meaning as the object."³³ That is, Tanabe sought to convey that the meaning a subject discovers in nature is actualized through their own decisions.

The philosophical-historical significance of self-conscious purposiveness lies in how it supplements Kant's moral theory, addressing the inadequacies of its formalism, as critiqued by Hegel. It is made evident by Tanabe's remark that his attempt is "to reconfigure the formalistic ethical theory of the second *Critique* through the teleological perspective of the third *Critique*, thereby concretizing the former via the latter as contentism [内容主義]."³⁴ That is, by utilizing self-conscious purposiveness, Tanabe sought to ground Kant's formalistic ethics in content as "contentism" or "non-formalism," thereby *constructing a moral theory that goes beyond Kant while remaining rooted in his philosophy.*

Tanabe's efforts culminate in the idea that "the practical reason of morality is not limited to the ability for a formal moral law without content, but also includes the ability for cognition of a moral law that contains as its content absolute negative purposiveness as 'purposiveness without purpose.'"³⁵ Examining the content of purposiveness realized in self-conscious purposiveness—the content that supplements Kant's formalistic ethics—Tanabe identifies this as Kant's concept of "purposiveness without purpose" (*Zweckmäßigkeit ohne Zweck*) found in the *Critique of Judgment*. Tanabe interprets this as "purposiveness as harmony,"³⁶ proposing that "the harmony of the whole, without any particular purpose, is itself the purpose."³⁷ This is "a purposiveness that regards the whole as the purpose"³⁸ and "must not be a purposiveness that assigns a purpose to anything within the realm

---

32. THZ 3:16.
33. THZ 3:48.
34. THZ 3:79.
35. THZ 6:42.
36. THZ 3:16.
37. THZ 3:413.
38. THZ 3:413.

of existence."[39] Thus, those who adopt the standpoint of self-conscious purposiveness must strive to realize "purposiveness *without* purpose" rather than "purposiveness *with* purpose." This entails making "the harmony of the whole"[40] their own purpose and acting as beings who, "through dialectical freedom, realize the teleological necessity of ought."[41]

Here, the world as a whole is understood as existing under harmony, necessitating actions aligned with the inevitable development of that harmony. For this reason, Tanabe describes self-conscious purposiveness as "the perfectly concrete combination of necessity and freedom."[42] Within this teleological worldview, individuals must choose whether to align with or resist the flow of purposive harmony. When one accepts this perspective and practices moral action according to teleological necessity, a self-conscious subject emerges, actively recognizing (or becoming conscious of) purposiveness without purpose. This is why Tanabe describes self-conscious purposiveness as "the purposiveness of the whole natural world as attributed from the perspective of human beings as moral agents."[43]

In connection with the previous section, purposiveness without purpose forms the content of "goodness" in improving society. The "goodness" necessary for improving society manifests as part of an individual's self-consciousness. It is precisely this self-consciousness that enables individuals to improve society.

The concept of self-conscious purposiveness was later integrated into the absolute dialectic in 1929, leading to the proposition that individuals not only find meaning in the overarching operation of the world but also participate in its realization through moral praxis. This idea is evident in Tanabe's assertion in *Hegelian Philosophy and Dialectic* that his standpoint "emphasizes teleological, moral praxis."[44] Naturally, this became a fundamental idea of the logic of species.

However, what ultimately validates the truth or falsehood of this self-consciousness? While absolute knowledge and purposiveness without purpose are established as guiding principles, how can they avoid being dismissed as subjective ideals or mere doxa? From the perspective of Tanabe's

39. THZ 3:104.
40. THZ 3:413.
41. THZ 3:210.
42. THZ 3:48.
43. THZ 3:18.
44. THZ 3:82.

failed logic of species and his subsequent reconstruction of philosophy as metanoetics, one could argue that *it is precisely this self-conscious purposiveness, grounded in trust in reason, that led Tanabe's philosophy toward totalitarianism.* Next, we will examine the problematic aspects inherent in the concept of self-conscious purposiveness.

3. THE LIMIT OF HUMAN IDEAL: A CRITIQUE OF SELF-CONSCIOUS PURPOSIVENESS

Let us start with an obvious premise: we are finite beings with limited capabilities. For instance, to paraphrase Sartre, we cannot simultaneously engage in "caring for an ill parent" and "joining the war for our homeland." Both actions are beneficial to someone, and yet we can only choose one as our course of action. Let us call this condition "fundamental finitude."

Our fundamental finitude accompanies us in virtually all our actions. When we attempt to realize some societal ideal, if the available choices are mutually exclusive, we can only select one of them. For example, "increasing the consumption tax to expand the national budget for public works" and "lowering the consumption tax to raise citizens' income" create an antinomy. The former enhances national infrastructure and social welfare, while the latter enriches individuals' lives—both contribute to public welfare. In this sense, both policies can be proven "right," much like how Kant demonstrated the antinomies of reason. It is in the very ability to prove this "rightness" in their respective ways that the "violence of reason," as proposed in this chapter, lies latent.

In order to proceed further, we turn to concrete examples. Consider the premise that "killing another person is an evil act," a notion that many, including the author, would agree with in an ordinary society. It goes without saying that a society where people can live in safety requires mutual agreement not to kill one another. To achieve this peaceful society desired by the majority, it may—though extreme—be necessary to exclude individuals who "can find meaning in life only by killing others." This could involve treating such individuals as "insane" and incarcerating them or deterring them through measures such as capital punishment for those who commit murder. Here emerges the idea of "killing those who kill others." In other words, it reflects a pure form of quantitative utilitarianism: achieving a peaceful society for the majority by depriving a minority of pleasure-driven killers of their freedom. This is an exclusionary stance that realizes a peaceful society by excluding the latter.

Of course, such extreme examples may be justifiable under an exclusionary stance. Furthermore, there might be no truly conflicting antinomy between "killing is good" and "killing is evil." Now, let us consider an example where the conflict appears more balanced. As with the previous example, many people would agree with the premise that pursuing altruistic actions benefiting others or society is not inherently wrong. However, what happens when such actions are regarded as duties? For instance, as seen in many religious traditions, donation is often considered a good deed or even an obligation. Yet does the inverse—that "not donating" is an evil action—hold true? If the societal norm "donation is a duty" were established as strongly as the idea that "killing is evil," would those who do not donate be seen as morally inferior?

Indeed, "donation is a duty" is not enshrined in law (at least in Japan known to the author), so failure to fulfill this would not result in legal penalties. However, in a society where donations become the norm, those who do not donate may face some form of social sanction. Such sanctions might be justified by religious precepts or social norms. In this sense, all communities—including religious orders—possess an inherent tendency to exclude individuals who deviate from established social norms, even if those norms are generally considered "good." Accordingly, attempts to make society "better" lead to coercion or exclusion of those who do not adhere to the defined "goodness." This is the "violence of reason" proposed in this chapter.

Considering Tanabe's logic of species in this context reveals its achievement in attributing two dimensions to societal "goodness": "social goodness" and "rational goodness." The "self-conscious purposiveness" discussed in the previous section forms the basis for the latter, while the core concept of the logic of species—"species" (or species substratum [種的基体])—grounds the former goodness. Let us clarify the meaning of this concept and its difference from self-conscious purposiveness.

Much can be said about the concept of the species, but for this chapter, we limit the discussion to its relevant context.[45] In order to construct his social ontology in a logically rigorous manner, Tanabe reinterpreted Aristotle's categories of genus, species, and individual in his own way.[46] He

45. For detail, see Urai, "Tanabe Hajime's Social Ontology."
46. For the English expressions related to these categories, this section follows

transformed these categories from purely quantitative ones to qualitative categories, retaining their quantitative implications. Using this framework, he sought to explain literally all aspects of this world—from historical changes to the spin of subatomic particles. In terms of social ontology, genus, species, and individual correspond to humanity, society, and the individual, respectively. All communities between the entirety of humanity and the individual—including families, towns, cities, nations, and even broader classifications such as Europe, Asia, and America—are categorized as species. This structure retains the quantitative aspect within the framework.

The qualitative aspect of genus, species, and individual, in the context of social ontology, is determined by whether the species and individual possess the nature of the genus (expressed as "humane character" [人類性]). While Tanabe's focus in social ontology was on elucidating the relationship between society (species) and the individual (individual), his goal was for both the species and the individual to acquire a humane character. In other words, he aimed to realize a "genus species" (類的種)[47] and a "genus individual" (類的個)[48] from given societies and individuals. This process is called the "generification" (類化) or "rationalization" of species and individual. Practically, this means a society and individuals capable of coexisting with other societies and nations. Amid the actuality of war and conflicts with other nations, Tanabe's logic of species sought the ideal of a state capable of coexistence and the method for its construction.

Returning to the distinction between "social goodness" and "rational goodness," Tanabe attributed the former to species and the latter to genus. He argued that "species-based goodness" is rationalized into "genus-based goodness" through a process grounded in his "trust in reason." However, "species-based goodness" may include irrational or immoral practices—such as bullying—if they serve the interests of the majority within a given group.

What about the earlier example of donations? At first glance, donations appear moral and might therefore be classified under genus. However, the distinction is not so clear cut—moral actions are not automatically placed in genus. In such cases, genus functions as the antithesis of species while remaining within the same dimension. As a higher-order category,

---

Tanabe, "Third Stage of Ontology." For details, see its "Issues of Translation" (368–71).

47. THZ 6:305.
48. THZ 6:132.

genus ultimately legitimizes the process by which species is rationalized and generalized.

This difference in dimensions raises a crucial question: What is the structural difference between persecution in the form of bullying and the persecution of those who refuse to donate? Simply being rational or moral stands in opposition to the irrational or immoral, but this opposition alone does not establish definitive goodness. Nevertheless, those who "trust in reason" would instinctively side with the rational or moral, which is precisely where Tanabe's notion of "trust in reason" falters. The failure of the logic of species thus emerges as an inevitable consequence of war, where "obedience to the commands of the state" came to be seen as the realization of human freedom.[49] Within this framework, the *state*—regarded as the foundation supporting the *lives of many*—demanded that *individuals* make *personal* sacrifices to preserve it.

By linking Tanabe's failure to self-conscious purposiveness, we can further this examination. Self-conscious purposiveness forms the content of "genus-based goodness," which, in Tanabe's logic of species, serves as absolute knowledge. Since it belongs to a higher order than "species-based goodness," practicing it is expected to improve society. However, our actions, constrained by fundamental finitude, always risk falling into contradiction. No matter how refined, "goodness" can only ever be better, never absolutely good. As a result, even knowledge designated as absolute knowledge retains only relative goodness. Because all goodness is relative, we cannot determine whether a moral action belongs to species or genus. This uncertainty is evident in the example of bullying within a group and in Tanabe's own philosophical missteps. Consequently, the content of self-conscious purposiveness remains highly ambiguous. This ambiguity was a fundamental flaw in the logic of species, and by 1936, Tanabe was already on the threshold of totalitarianism, asserting that *"the power of the state must be the forceful coercion of the ethical."*[50]

This problem becomes apparent when examining cases such as the pleasure-driven killer or bullying. But what about moral actions such as donations? When donations are framed as a duty—an ought—how do they differ from the "forceful coercion of the ethical"? Tanabe's concept of the species substratum has the potential to justify all social ideals, regardless of their nature. What guarantees that a person who judges others morally is not

---

49. THZ 7:41.
50. THZ 6:374; emphasis added.

merely a puppet controlled by the coercive force of the species substratum? The question of what makes society better inevitably leads to antinomy, leaving us unable to determine what is truly better. Here lies the "inescapable fate of reason"[51] that awaits all those who seek to improve society.

However, if we were to end here, only despair would remain. As long as we aspire to be moral and desire to improve society, there must be something that fulfills that wish. Otherwise, we would be left with a choice between hesitating at our own violence and doing nothing, or straightforwardly embracing it and acting upon our desires. This is where the significance of Tanabe's development of absolute nothingness into "nothingness-sive-love" (無即愛) and the expansion of reason's "philosophy of self-power" into a "philosophy of Other-power," which "transcends rational intuition,"[52] becomes clear. Next, we examine this philosophy with the Absolute.

4. FROM A PHILOSOPHY OF THE ABSOLUTE TO A PHILOSOPHY WITH THE ABSOLUTE

In *Philosophy as Metanoetics*, Tanabe consistently discusses the impotence of reason to attain the truth on its own. However, this does not mean that he abandoned the pursuit of absolute knowledge—at least not in this work. Rather, Tanabe shifts from the stance of acquiring absolute knowledge through self-power to receiving it as a gift from the Absolute. Tanabe names the philosophy born of reason's acknowledgment of its own impotence as "metanoetics" (懺悔道), but he still insists that "metanoetics itself is absolute knowledge."[53] In *Philosophy as Metanoetics*, the attainment of absolute knowledge is described as follows:

> If it is possible in any sense for us to attain absolute knowledge and practice it, this must involve not a self-power ascent but a turning enabled by the descent of Other-power, which mediates the transformation of the relative into the absolute.[54]

The failure of the logic of species lies in its inability to demonstrate anything "absolutely right" through rational speculation; instead, it merely results in endless disputes over "better" alternatives. This limitation was

---

51. THZ 9:52.
52. THZ 9:18.
53. THZ 9:36.
54. THZ 9:37.

obscured by Tanabe's reliance on self-conscious purposiveness and trust in reason, ultimately culminating in the "forceful coercion of the ethical."[55] For those who abandon this path, improving society through rationally derived "good" becomes impossible, as such "good" is always relative—merely "better" within a comparative framework. Consequently, the path to absolute knowledge through self-power is already closed.

If philosophy remains possible—and particularly if a philosophy capable of addressing absolute knowledge is possible—its foundation must be demonstrated apart from human effort. Here, Tanabe introduces the concept of the Absolute as nothingness-sive-love. Absolute knowledge is no longer "knowledge *about the Absolute*" sought from our side but instead becomes "knowledge *bestowed by the Absolute*" in moments of paralysis before antinomies. Philosophy grounded in this knowledge becomes Tanabe's new philosophy: a philosophy of religion as philosophy as metanoetics.

The Absolute in this new philosophy is characterized as enabling "the paradox of not allowing deadlocks to remain as such."[56] More specifically, it "treats me, entirely impotent and always deviating from the right way, as if I were able to walk the right way, making me act as if I were fully capable, even though I am far from it."[57] In Tanabe's earlier works, the logic of species upheld rational activity grounded in self-conscious purposiveness as the sole way to improve society. However, after confronting the fundamental impossibility of this approach, such a method can no longer be sustained. Instead, the Absolute—the one who saves even those rendered powerless in the deadlock of antinomies—emerges at the center of Tanabe's thought. This Absolute, equated with the "principle of dialectic,"[58] is experienced by the saved as the love of the Absolute in a religious sense. Termed "nothingness-sive-love," absolute nothingness in the logic of species develops into a savior in the philosophy as metanoetics. The salvation by nothingness-sive-love is expressed as follows:

> When one resolves to die willingly in the middle of an antinomy, the gate to the middle way—neither the thesis nor the antithesis—unexpectedly opens.[59]

---

55. THZ 6:374.
56. Tanabe, *Philosophy as Metanoetics*, 19.
57. Tanabe, *Philosophy as Metanoetics*, 19–20.
58. THZ 9:471.
59. THZ 9:233.

The resolution of an antinomy is not an either-or decision but a higher resolution granted as a middle way: a neither-nor granted by the Absolute in response to the antinomies one faces. Thus, the content of absolute knowledge consists of this singular neither-nor, bestowed by the Absolute.

Salvation in philosophy as metanoetics is not a resignation to social absurdities or the impotence of reason. Rather, it must render improving society possible once more. Yet, this raises a critical question: What is the nature of this new absolute knowledge granted by the Absolute? Tanabe describes it as follows: "Something is always presented to me with the words, 'Surely, you can at least do *this*. Try it.'"[60] In other words, the Absolute provides something practicable—distinct from the agonizing choices of either-or. Regarding the content of this "*this*," Tanabe writes:

> From an external perspective, this may appear indistinguishable from the utilitarianism or pragmatism of relative calculation based on the discriminative reasoning of the understanding. However, its meaning is entirely different in the self-consciousness of the subject. This is because, at the extreme limit where discriminative understanding reaches an impasse and disintegrates, leading to the loss of self, one is resurrected by the Other-power of absolute nothingness, and because it is precisely in the content of the praxis, led to as an inescapable necessity of absolute actuality, that the Absolute is testified to.[61]

Praxis as absolute knowledge ultimately manifests in the most ordinary acts of everyday life. Viewed externally, they may appear to be carried out with calculated intent. However, for the subject, these actions arise as the singular "this"—neither this nor that—an action that they are led to perform. For this reason, praxis as absolute knowledge cannot be judged subjectively as good or evil, nor can it be assessed as such by others; it possesses the quality appealed to in the statement "only God says that it is good."[62]

In conclusion, Tanabe's moral theory ultimately fails to provide substantive content to Kantian formalism, instead remaining subordinate to its framework. While Tanabe might claim that the singular "this" granted by the Absolute offers a response to formalism, this "this," emerging through antinomy, lacks concrete content and is defined solely by the specificities

---

60. Tanabe, *Philosophy as Metanoetics*, 19; emphasis added.
61. THZ 8:348.
62. THZ 9:344.

of each situational context, that is, formalism. Therefore, for those who acknowledge reason's impotence yet refuse to abandon the pursuit of societal improvement, the only remaining course of action lies in acts characterized exclusively by their form as being granted by the Absolute.[63]

CONCLUSION

Tanabe Hajime's philosophy traces a profound journey from rational idealism to a paradigm in which the limitations of reason serve as the gateway to absolute knowledge. In reconstructing the logic of species, Tanabe underscores the inherent shortcomings of self-conscious purposiveness. While it strives to improve society, it inevitably succumbs to the relative nature of its "better" alternatives, exposing the violence of reason—an antinomy in which every rational solution carries the potential for exclusion or coercion. Put differently, the violence of reason manifests in the effort to achieve something better by comparing A and B, or to prevent realizing something deemed inferior. This violence is an intrinsic feature of all communities—whether secular or religious—and of the individuals living within them. Tanabe's philosophy confronts the despair of this recognition, revealing how the pursuit of absolute goodness is thwarted by the finitude of reason.

The turning point in Tanabe's thought is his acknowledgment of the impotence of reason, leading to the philosophy of metanoetics. Here, absolute knowledge is no longer acquired through human effort but is bestowed by the Absolute—nothingness-sive-love—in the deadlock of antinomy. This reorientation from self-power to Other-power transforms his framework of rationality. The Absolute enables action not by resolving antinomies rationally but by granting a singular, non-dualistic "this" that transcends the antinomies of reason.

Actions informed by this knowledge are distinct from utilitarian calculations, even if they appear similar externally. For the subject, such actions arise as a response to an inevitable necessity, imbued with the transcendent meaning of being granted by the Absolute. This transformation allows for a reimagining of societal improvement, not as a rational imposition but as a praxis sustained by a profound relationality with the Absolute.

---

63. As for Tanabe's soteriology in detail, see Urai: "Faith and Knowledge"; "Shinran's Concept of *Jinen Honi*."

Ultimately, Tanabe's philosophy demonstrates that while reason's impotence is inescapable, it is not a terminus. Instead, it opens the door to a new mode of ethical engagement—one grounded in humility, openness to the transcendent, and the grace of the Absolute. This shift redefines the possibilities of human praxis, offering a path beyond the despair of reason's limitations.

BIBLIOGRAPHY

Hegel, G. W. F. *Elements of the Philosophy of Right*. Edited by Allen W. Wood. Translated by H. B. Nisbet. Rev. ed. Cambridge Texts in the History of Political Thought. Cambridge: Cambridge University Press, 1991.

Heisig, James W. *Philosophers of Nothingness: An Essay on the Kyoto School*. Nanzan Library of Asian Religion and Culture. Honolulu: University of Hawaii Press, 2001.

Morisato, Takeshi. *Tanabe Hajime and the Kyoto School: Self, World, and Knowledge*. Bloomsbury Introductions to World Philosophies. London: Bloomsbury Academic, 2022.

Nishida, Kitarō. 自覚に於ける直観と反省 [Intuition and reflection in self-consciousness]. Tokyo: Iwanami, 1917.

Sugimura, Yasuhiko. "Phenomenology Touching Its Limits: Tanabe and Levinas in 1934." In *Tetsugaku Companion to Phenomenology and Japanese Philosophy*, edited by Shigeru Taguchi and Andrea Altobrando, 113–28. Tetsugaku Companions to Japanese Philosophy 3. Cham, Switz.: Springer, 2019.

Takahashi, Satomi. *The Complete Works of Takahashi Satomi*. Vol. 7. Tokyo: Fukumura Shuppan, 1973.

Tanabe, Hajime. "On Thetic Judgement." Translated by Morten E. Jelby et al. *European Journal of Japanese Philosophy* 6 (2021) 227–40.

———. 懺悔道としての哲学：田辺元哲学選II [Philosophy as metanoetics: Selected works of Tanabe Hajime, vol. 2]. Edited by Masakatsu Fujita. Tokyo: Iwanami Shoten, 2010.

———. "The Third Stage of Ontology." Translated by Urai Satoshi and Sova P. K. Cerda. *European Journal of Japanese Philosophy* 7 (2022) 361–410.

Urai, Satoshi. "Faith and Knowledge in Tanabe Hajime's Philosophy of Religion." *European Journal of Japanese Philosophy* 5 (2020) 5–32.

———. "Shinran's Concept of *Jinen Honi* (Naturalness) from the Viewpoint of Tanabe Hajime's Philosophy of Religion." *Eastern Buddhist*, 3rd ser., 3 (2023) 67–85.

———. "Tanabe Hajime's Social Ontology: From the 'Logic of Species' to the 'Logic of Love.'" Translated by Sova P. K. Cerda. 『求真』 [*Kyūshin*] 27 (2022) 121–47.

7

Kenosis

A Dialogue Between Nicholas of Cusa and Nishitani Keiji

Myriam-Sonja Hantke

INTRODUCTION: WHAT IS KENOSIS?

The word κένωσις has its origin in the ancient Greek word κενόω. κένωσις can be translated as "becoming empty" or "alienation." However, the word κένωσις is not found in the New Testament, and the form κενόω only five times: Rom 4:14; 1 Cor 1:17; 9:15; 2 Cor 9:3; Phil 2:7. Of these, Phil 2:7 is the most significant passage. Here the verb appears in the third-person singular aorist indicative active and can be translated as "emptying oneself." In Phil 2:5–11 it is written:

> 5 Τοῦτο φρονεῖτε ἐν ὑμῖν ὃ καὶ ἐν Χριστῷ Ἰησοῦ, 6 ὃς ἐν μορφῇ θεοῦ ὑπάρχων οὐχ ἁρπαγμὸν ἡγήσατο τὸ εἶναι ἴσα θεῷ, 7 ἀλλ' ἑαυτὸν ἐκένωσεν μορφὴν δούλου λαβών, ἐν ὁμοιώματι ἀνθρώπων γενόμενος· καὶ σχήματι εὑρεθεὶς ὡς ἄνθρωπος 8 ἐταπείνωσεν ἑαυτὸν γενόμενος ὑπήκοος μέχρι θανάτου, θανάτου δὲ σταυροῦ. 9 διὸ καὶ ὁ θεὸς αὐτὸν ὑπερύψωσεν καὶ ἐχαρίσατο αὐτῷ τὸ ὄνομα τὸ ὑπὲρ πᾶν ὄνομα, 10 ἵνα ἐν τῷ ὀνόματι Ἰησοῦ πᾶν γόνυ κάμψῃ ἐπουρανίων καὶ ἐπιγείων καὶ

καταχθονίων 11 καὶ πᾶσα γλῶσσα ἐξομολογήσηται ὅτι κύριος Ἰησοῦς Χριστὸς εἰς δόξαν θεοῦ πατρός.

> 5 Have this mind among yourselves, which is yours in Christ Jesus, 6 who, though he was in the form of God, did not count equality with God a thing to be grasped, 7 but emptied himself, by taking the form of a servant, being born in the likeness of men. 8 And being found in human form, he humbled himself by becoming obedient to the point of death, even death on a cross. 9 Therefore God has highly exalted him and bestowed on him the name that is above every name, 10 so that at the name of Jesus every knee should bow, in heaven and on earth and under the earth, 11 and every tongue confess that Jesus Christ is Lord, to the glory of God the Father. (ESV)

Jesus Christ was equal to God, and he negated himself to become a human being. Finally, this self-negation led him to the death of Jesus Christ on the cross. Thereupon, in the resurrection of Jesus Christ, his exaltation and negation of his human nature took place, whereby he returned to God. In this μετάνοια God showed his own pain and at the same time his divine love.[1] As a sign of his divinity, God bestowed upon him the name of all names, that is, the name that transcends all names.

In my chapter I would like to consider the concept of kenosis in the philosophy of Nicholas of Cusa (1401–64) and Nishitani Keiji (1900–90). Is it not twofold? Is there not a first and a second kenosis? What does kenosis mean? An emptiness of being (Jesus Christ) or rather of nothingness (*nihilum*)? Finally, leads it not to a kenosis of kenosis in Nishitani's philosophy, which transcends the kenosis of Cusanus?

KENOSIS IN CHRISTIANITY: NICHOLAS OF CUSA[2]

2.1 The Mathematical Image of God

Nicholas of Cusa presented his philosophy in his main work *De Docta Ignorantia* (1440): In volume 1 Cusanus considers the absolute maximum

---

1. Kitamori, *Theologie des Schmerzes Gottes*.
2. Hantke, *Das Nicht-Andere*, 17–40. The following quotations are from Nicholas of Cusa: *On Learned Ignorance*.

(*maximum absolutum*) in his coincidence of opposites (*coincidentia oppositorum*).³ In volume 2 he unfolds a cosmology in which he presents the universe as a parable of the absolute maximality, which is the infolding (*complicatio*) and at the same time the unfolding (*explicatio*) of God, and in volume 3 his Christology with Jesus Christ as the absolute and contracted maximum (*maximum absolutum et contractum*).

According to Cusanus, God in his non-otherness can be seen by his creatures only through a mirror.⁴ For him, mathematics is the method that seems most suitable to lead people to God as the absolute maximum.⁵ According to Haubst, Cusanus thus develops a "mathematical mysticism," a mysticism that is described mathematically.⁶ Since the absolute maximum cannot be larger or smaller, it coincides with the absolute minimum.⁷ That's why Cusanus can say that God encompasses everything as the absolute maximum and minimum. Cusanus illustrates it by using various geometric figures: he shows that the infinite line (unlimited) coincides with an infinite triangle (limited) and this with a circle or a sphere (curved).⁸ By this way he shows that the infinite line is identical to the different geometric shapes and symbolizes God, who is all in all (1 Cor 15:28). The infinite triangle symbolizes the Trinity, the infinite circle the divine unity, and the infinite sphere the absolute being of God.⁹ However, since the universe in its maximality, does not represent the absolute maximum, and there is no perfect individual without limitations immanent in the world, leads Cusanus to his third book. Here, Cusanus considers Jesus Christ as the absolute and contracted maximum and develops a Christology as kenosis.

---

3. According to Stallmach, three motives can be distinguished with regard to the *coincidence of opposites (coincidentia oppositorum)*: (1) unity over multiplicity (ontological-metaphysical motive), (2) insight over understanding (gnoseological motive), and (3) God over unity and multiplicity, about insight and understanding (mystical-theological motive) (*Ineinsfall der Gegensätze*, 1–36). See also Flasch, *Nikolaus von Kues*, 44–70.

4. Hopkins, *Nicholas of Cusa*, 1.11.30 (HAA 1:22).

5. Haubst, *Bild*, 203–99.

6. Haubst, *Bild*, 293–99.

7. Hopkins, *Nicholas of Cusa*, 1.4.11 (HAA 1:10).

8. Hopkins, *Nicholas of Cusa*, 1.14.37–1.15.41 (HAA 1:27–30).

9. Hopkins, *Nicholas of Cusa*, 1.19.55–1.23.70 (HAA 1:37–44).

2.2 Jesus Christ and the First Kenosis

Cusanus dedicates his work to Cardinal Julian, to whom, after his doctrine of God in the first book and his cosmology in the second book, he now presents his Christology in the third book, which is basically a mathematical-theological commentary on Phil 2:5–11. The method is the *learned ignorance* that Cusanus had already developed in his first book. The absolute maximum (God) can be recognized only in a conjectural way. After Cusanus showed in his second book that the universe represents a contracted maximum (*contractum absolutum*) in its plurality, he emphasizes that it lacks the unity of the maximum in an absolute way. Beings differ in their degrees of type and number, which means that every being stands between the maximum and the minimum and has a specific degree of limitation. The limited being can never become identical with the absolute maximum.[10] God is the origin, center, and goal and therefore the whereupon of the universe and of all limited individual beings.[11] Cusanus shows that the cosmos exists in a limited way and multiplicity. But the contracted maximum cannot exist without an absolute maximum. If this were a human individual, according to Cusanus, it would be characterized by the greatest perfection and would therefore be the true foundation of all things.[12] This contracted maximum is not only limited, but also God at the same time:

> And here from it is evident—in conformity with the points I exhibited a bit earlier—that the contracted maximum [individual] cannot exist as purely contracted. For no such [purely contracted thing] could attain the fullness of perfection in the genus of its contraction. Nor would such a thing qua contracted be God, who is most absolute. But, necessarily, the contracted maximum [individual]—i.e., God and creature—would be both absolute and contracted, by virtue of a contraction which would be able to exist in itself only if it existed in Absolute Maximality.[13]

---

10. Hopkins, *Nicholas of Cusa*, 3.1.183 (HAA 1:119).
11. Hopkins, *Nicholas of Cusa*, 3.1.185 (HAA 1:120).
12. Hopkins, *Nicholas of Cusa*, 3.2.191 (HAA 1:124).

13. "Et ex hoc manifestum est ipsum maximum contractum non posse ut pure contractum subsistere, secundum e aquae paulo ante ostendimus, cum nullum tale plenitudinem perfectionis in genere contractionis attingere possit. Neque etiam ipsum tale ut contractum deus, qui est absolutissimus, esset; sed necessario foret maximum contractum, hoc est deus et creatura, absolutum et contractum, contractione quae in se subsistere non posset nisi in absoluta maximitate subsistente" (Kues, *Belehrte Unwissenheit*, 3.2.192 [HAA 1:124]).

There exists nothing greater than this in a limited way and, conversely, it forms the maximum of the limited. This contracted maximum is identical with the absolute maximum and is creator and creature, absolute and contracted at the same time. In other words: it is the *contracted absolute*. However, the unity of the absolute and the contracted individual must not be understood in its difference, since there is no difference in the absolute.[14] In the contracted maximum, the absolute and the contracted are one.[15] According to Cusanus, this contracted maximum is only possible in man.[16] However, this cannot be an ordinary human being in his finitude, but only a human being who is a true human being and a true God at the same time.[17] This one is: *Jesus Christ*.[18] Cusanus refers to the Council of Chalcedon, at which it was said that in Jesus Christ both natures are without mixture, without composition, and without separation. Jesus Christ was a true God and a true human being at the same time. In him both natures are united and at the same time distinguished. Cusanus follows Paul, who showed that in Jesus Christ lies all perfection, the redemption and forgiveness of sins:

> He is the Image of the Invisible God, the Firstborn of all creation because in Him all things were created, in heaven and on earth, visible and invisible, whether thrones or dominions or principalities or powers; all things were created through Him and in Him; and He is prior to all things, and in Him all things exist. And He is the head of the body, the church; He is the Beginning, the Firstborn from the dead, so that He holds the primacy in all respects. For it was pleasing that all fullness dwell in Him and that through Him all things be reconciled unto Him. (Col 1:14–20)[19]

Jesus Christ is the image of God and the firstborn of all creation. He is before all creation and the fullness of all creation (Phil 2:6–11; Col 1:15–20).

---

14. Hopkins, *Nicholas of Cusa*, 3.2.193 (HAA 1:124).
15. Hopkins, *Nicholas of Cusa*, 3.2.194 (HAA 1:125).
16. Hopkins, *Nicholas of Cusa*, 3.3.198 (HAA 1:127).
17. "I and the Father are one" (John 10:30).
18. Hopkins, *Nicholas of Cusa*, 3.4.203 (HAA 1:129).
19. Translated from Cusanus: "Qui est imago dei invisibilis, primogenitus omnis creaturae, quia in ipso condita sunt universa in caelis et in terra, visibilia et invisibilia, sive throni sive dominations sive principatus sive potestas: omnia per ipsum et in ipso create sunt, et ipse est ante omnes, et omnia in ipso constant. Et ipse est caput corporis ecclesiae, qui est principium, primogenitus ex mortuis, ut sit in omnibus ipse primatum tenens; quia in ipso complacuit omnem plenitudinem inhabitare et per eum reconciliari omnia in ipsum" (Kues, *Belehrte Unwissenheit*, 3.4.203 [HAA 1:129]).

He is also the head of the church (Rom 12:4–5; 1 Cor 12:12–27) and the firstborn from the dead (Col 1:18). In everything, Jesus Christ has primacy and so transcends everything that exists. Since he unites both sides—true God and true human being—he can reconcile everything with himself and free people from their sins.[20] This reconciliation through Jesus Christ does not happen in the beings, but rather in and through Jesus Christ, in whom they possess their being in the highest fullness.

This reconciliation involves a twofold mystery, that is, the death and the resurrection of Jesus Christ. God is the absolute maximum who, in his development, created the universe and man as limited entities. Jesus Christ is the contracted maximum, who negates and empties himself into the limited human being. After his death on the cross he resurrects and returns to the absolute maximum. Therefore, Jesus Christ shows his power over life and death. Kenosis does not mean that Jesus Christ negates himself and is a mere nothing. Here he gets his true being:

> Therefore, since God is in all things in such way that all things are in Him, it is evident that God—in equality of being all things and without any change in Himself—exists in oneness with the maximum humanity of Jesus; for the maximum human nature can exist in God only maximally. And so, in Jesus, who is the Equality of being all things, the Eternal Father and the Eternal Holy Spirit exist (just as they exist in God-the-Son, who is the middle person); and [in Jesus], just as in the Word, all things [exist]; and every creature [exists] in the supreme and most perfect humanity, which completely enfolds all creatable things. Thus, all fullness dwells in Jesus.[21]

In other words: only through kenosis, where God negates and empties himself in Jesus Christ, Jesus Christ gets his true being. In him, being and nothingness are united with each other. Therefore, Jesus Christ is able to redeem our sins for us.

---

20. Hopkins, *Nicholas of Cusa*, 3.4.204 (HAA 1:130).

21. "Et ita in Iesu, qui sic est aequalitas omnia essendi, tamquam in filio in divinis, qui est media persona, pater aeternus et sanctus spiritus exsistunt, et omnia ut in verbo, et omnis creatura in ipsa humanitate summa et perfectissima universaliter omnia creabilia complicanti, ut sit omnis plenitude ipsum inhabitans" (Kues, *Belehrte Unwissenheit*, 3.4.204 [HAA 1:131]).

2.3 Jesus Christ and the Second Kenosis

However, the kenosis of Jesus Christ is incomplete if you look only to the first kenosis (incarnation of Jesus Christ). It is followed by a second kenosis, that is, the death on the cross and the resurrection of Jesus Christ. However, humans cannot understand this *kenotic mystery* of death and resurrection of Jesus Christ. Humans are unable to understand something which is transcendent and divine at the same time.[22] For humans the sensual has always priority over the spirit.[23] In other words: people live only in a sensual world and cannot transcend it to the spiritual world. By turning to the sensual, people do not only turn away from the spiritual, but especially from God himself, and thus towards sin and evil. Although sin has its origins in the first parents, it is also ontologically based in the striving of the spirit for autonomy.[24] Humans cannot free themselves from their turn to the sensual and evil, but only Jesus Christ is able to kenotically elevate them from the sensual to the spiritual world (Rom 7:25a).[25] Cusanus writes:

> Except for Christ Jesus, who descended from Heaven, there was never anyone who had [enough] power over himself and over his own nature (which in its origin is so subject to the sins of carnal desire) to be able, of himself, to ascend beyond his own origin to eternal and heavenly things. Jesus is the one who ascended by His own power and in whom the human nature (begotten not from the will of the flesh but from God) was not hindered from mightily returning to God the Father.[26]

In contrast to human beings, who are bound to the world of the senses, Jesus Christ is able to free himself from it and to transcend his true humanity to his true divinity. This is the *second kenosis* of Jesus Christ. He descended into the sensual and sinful world and ascended to the divine Father. Since Jesus Christ represents the true divinity and the true humanity in a highest

---

22. Hopkins, *Nicholas of Cusa*, 3.6.216 (HAA 1:136).
23. Hopkins, *Nicholas of Cusa*, 3.6.217 (HAA 1:137).
24. Haubst, *Christologie des Nikolaus*, 63–73.
25. Stallmach, *Ineinsfall der Gegensätze*, 99–119.
26. "Nemo umquam fuit ex se potens supra se ipsum ac propriam suam naturam ita peccatis desideria carnalis originaliter subditam posse ascendere supra suam radicem ad aeterna et caelestia, nisi qui de caelo descendit Christus Iesus. Hic est, qui et propria virtute ascendit, in quo ipsa humana natura non ex voluntate carnis, sed ex deo nata nihil obstaculi habuit, quin et potenter ad deum patrem redirect" (Kues, *Belehrte Unwissenheit*, 3.6.218 [HAA 1:137]).

degree, he can transcend the sensual world of life and death. By this way he can free the human beings from their sins and the evil. The death on the cross of Jesus Christ denotes the second kenosis:

> The man Christ's voluntary and most innocent, most shameful, and most cruel death on the Cross was the deletion and purgation of, and the satisfaction for, all the carnal desires of human nature. Whatever humanly can be done counter to the love for a neighbor is abundantly made up for in the fullness of Christ's love, by which He delivered Himself unto death even on behalf of His enemies.[27]

Through the death on the cross, Jesus Christ could free humans from their sins and reconciled them with God. Jesus Christ was able to do this because in him the contracted and the absolute maximum are connected in an absolute love. This *kenotic love* characterizes Jesus Christ. The reconciliation through the death on the cross of Jesus Christ is, on the one hand, the reconciliation of people with the good and the spirit or God, and on the other hand, the reconciliation with other people in true love. This shows the *double commandment of love*: love for God and love for one's neighbor (Mark 12:29–31). This reconciliation through Jesus Christ is achieved only by those who are one with Jesus Christ, but the differences of the beings are preserved.[28] Kenotic reconciliation does not occur equally for all people, but rather gradually. The more a person is united with Jesus Christ in a kenotic love, the more he participates in this reconciliation. In this reconciliation, the cross of Jesus Christ becomes the cross of humanity, whereby humans themselves experience the kenosis and are thereby justified. This justification does not come by human power, but rather by the grace of God. The mystery of the cross lies in the fact that the spiritual transcends the sensual and Jesus Christ, who is the most perfect human being, voluntarily accepts the death of the cross in order to reconcile humans with himself in communion with God. Through the resurrection, Jesus Christ was able to return to his Father by transforming his mortal nature into the immortal nature through death and performing a second kenosis:[29]

---

27. "Voluntaria et innocentissima, turpissima atque crudelissima hominis Christi crucis mors omnium carnalium desideriorum humanae naturae extinctio, satisfaction atque purgation fuit. Quidquid humaniter contra caritatem proximi fieri potest, in plenitudine caritatis Christi, qua se ipsum morti etiam dedit pro inimicis, habundanter exstat adimpletum" (Kues, *Belehrte Unwissenheit*, 3.6.218 [HAA 1:137–38]).

28. Hopkins, *Nicholas of Cusa*, 3.6.219 (HAA 1:138).

29. Hopkins, *Nicholas of Cusa*, 3.7.221 (HAA 1:139).

> I must now say the following: since it was not fitting for human nature to be led to the triumph of immortality otherwise than through victory over death, [Christ] underwent death in order that human nature would rise again with Him to eternal life and that the animal, mortal body would become spiritual and incorruptible. [Christ] was able to be a true man only if He was mortal; and He was able to lead mortal [human] nature to immortality only if through death human nature became stripped of mortality.[30]

Jesus Christ was mortal as a true human being. However, he could kenotically negate his mortality only by transforming his human nature into immortality through death. In order to defeat mortality, he accepted death so that the mortal body transformed into an immortal, spiritual body. Cusanus refers to John 12:24, where Jesus Christ says that if the grain of wheat does not fall into the ground and die, it will remain alone.[31] On the other hand, if it dies, then it bears much fruit. This is also the case with the death of Jesus Christ: only by taking death upon himself and emptying himself of human nature he could lead the people to salvation. In other words: only through death could he reconcile the true humanity and the true divinity, whereby Jesus Christ in his true humanity was never separated from the true divinity. Therefore, body and soul were united with each other. A separation of body and soul could come only through the death, where body and soul were separated at the hour of death on the cross.[32] After the death on the cross, soul and body were reunited in the infinite, spiritual nature, that is, in the resurrection of Jesus Christ. This resurrection is at the same time the reconciliation of the two natures in Jesus Christ:

> Therefore, discern keenly: with respect to the fact that the humanity of Jesus is considered as contracted to the man Christ, it is likewise understood to be united also with His divinity. As united with the divinity, [the humanity] is fully absolute; [but] as it is considered to be that true man Christ, [the humanity] is contracted, so that Christ is a man through the humanity. And so, Jesus's humanity is as a medium between what is purely absolute and what

---

30. "Quoniam aliter humanam naturam ad immortalitas triumphum quam per mortis victoriam transduci non conveniebat, hinc mortem subiit, ut secum resurgeret humana natura ad vitam perpetuam, et animale mortale corpus fieret spirituale incorruptibile. Non potuit verus homo esse nisi mortalis, et non potuit ad immortalitatem mortalem naturam vehere nisi spoliate mortalitate per mortem" (Kues, *Belehrte Unwissenheit*, 3.7.221 [HAA 1:139]).

31. Hopkins, *Nicholas of Cusa*, 3.7.222 (HAA 1:139).

32. Hopkins, *Nicholas of Cusa*, 3.7.224 (HAA 1:140).

is purely contracted. Accordingly, then, it was corruptible only in a given respect; but absolutely it was incorruptible. Therefore, it was corruptible according to temporality, to which it was contracted; but in accordance with the fact that it was free from time, beyond time, and united with the divinity, it was incorruptible.[33]

Cusanus shows here again that in Jesus Christ both natures—the true humanity and the true divine nature—are united. As a true man he is mortal; as a true divinity he is immortal. This unity of true humanity and true divinity led to the resurrection of Jesus Christ, where he negated (emptied) his mortal nature and got a spiritual body. With this in mind, it can be said that Jesus Christ is the firstborn among all beings.[34] No one could arise before him, since no one is united with the absolute maximum like Jesus Christ. Since there is only one undivided humanity, all people will be resurrected together with Jesus Christ and fulfill the second kenosis:

> Therefore, it is evident that the following inference holds: the man Christ arose; hence, after [the cessation of] all motion of temporal corruptibility, all men will arise through Him, so that they will be eternally incorruptible.[35]

KENOSIS IN ZEN BUDDHISM: NISHITANI KEIJI

3.1 Nihilism and Modern Science

The starting point of Nishitani's *philosophy of emptiness* (Skrt. *śūnyatā*; Jap. *kū* 空) is: *nihilism*.[36] In a short essay, "Mein philosophischer Ausgangspunkt" (My philosophical starting point) from 1964, Nishitani writes:

---

33. "Humanitas enim Iesu ipso quod ad hominem Christum contracta consideratur, eo ipso etiam divinitati unita simul intelligatur. Cui ut unita est, plurimum absoluta est; ut consideratur Christus verus homo ille, contracta est, ut per humanitatem homo sit. Et ita humanitas Iesu es tut medium inter pure absolutum et pure contractum. Secundum hoc itaque non fuit corruptibilis nisi secundum quid, et simpliciter incorruptibilis" (Kues, *Belehrte Unwissenheit*, 3.7.225 [HAA 1:141]). See also Kues, *De Pace Fidei*, c.12.

34. Hopkins, *Nicholas of Cusa*, 3.8.227 (HAA 1:142).

35. "Christus homo resurrexit; hinc omnes homines resurgent per ipsum post omnem temporalis corruptibilitatis motum, ut sint perpetuo incorruptibiles" (Kues, *Belehrte Unwissenheit*, 3.8.227 [HAA 1:143]).

36. Hantke: *Mystik im Deutschen Idealismus*, 147–58; *Das Nicht-Andere*, 99–111.

> My starting point is none other than that of nihilism.[37]

For Nishitani, nihilism is the starting point of his philosophy: the *nihilum* is the standpoint of the European modernity, which must be transcended towards the field of emptiness. This can be understood as a kenosis, where the *nihilum* is emptied itself into emptiness.

In his book *Religion and Nothingness* (*Shūkyō to wa nanika* [宗教とは何か]; Germ. *Was ist Religion?*) from 1954–55, which is one of his major works, European nihilism is overcome to the field of emptiness. Nishitani describes this emptiness as the *true self-identity*, with which Nishitani establishes an *existential philosophy of emptiness*. For Nishitani, the problem of religion and science is one of the fundamental problems of modernity. The *nihilum* or nothingness of modern European nihilism is the methodological starting point for his philosophy of emptiness, in which he tries to make clear the relationship of religion and science. He emphasizes that if you separate both—religion and science—with a line, this line separates and connects them at the same time. The problem lies in determining this boundary line and the question of what it is.

A prejudice lies in the fact that (natural) science tries to describe nature objectively using natural laws and theories, whereas religion has only subjective truths of belief. Therefore, religion and science are opposed to each other. If you look at science, you can see that it grounds on indubitable natural laws, which form the basis for technology and the freedom of humanity.

At the same time, however, its reversal also emerges: because people also become slaves of technology, in which the laws of nature rule over people, which is reflected in the rationalization of human life and thinking. In the age of Enlightenment (*Aufklärung*), this was considered as a progress of humanity. However, upon closer consideration, it becomes clear that this is exactly what opens up the meaninglessness of human life or the abyss of the *nihilum*. Therefore, the progress appears as a step backwards. At the extreme limit of human freedom, humans themselves become mechanized and lose their human nature. Nishitani cites the example of nuclear weapons, because it shows this problem in a clear way. In modern times of despair and meaninglessness (arbitrariness), science or technology cannot give people answers to the ultimate metaphysical questions of thinking and being. To do this, another level must be entered. This is the level of *śūnyatā* (emptiness), on which humans and everything around them find their own suchness:

---

37. Nishitani, "Mein philosophischer Ausgangspunkt," 546.

Śūnyatā is the point at which we become manifest in our own suchness as concrete human beings, as individuals with both body and personality. And at the same time, it is the point at which everything around us becomes manifest in its own suchness.[38]

3.2 *Nihilum* and Emptiness (*Śūnyatā*) or the First and Second Kenosis

The (modern) *nihilum* is not the true nothingness or emptiness (*śūnyatā*), since humanity not yet freed themselves from the objectification of nothingness into a thing, nor from the radical subjectification of nothingness. Therefore, the *nihilum* must be negated in a kenotical way. If the *nihilum* is brought to its own true ground beyond subject-object duality, then the field of true emptiness opens up beyond being and nothingness, where humans and all things find their own suchness. Therefore, emptiness is the ground of the suchness of humans and all things. Nishitani emphasizes that emptiness is not an "entity":

> Emptiness in the sense of *śūnyatā* is emptiness only when it empties itself even of the standpoint that represents it as some "thing" that is emptiness. It is, in its original Form, self-emptying. In this meaning, true emptiness is not to be posited as something outside of and other than "being." Rather, it is to be realized as something united to and self-identical with being.[39]

The first kenosis from *nihilum* to emptiness must be followed by a *second* kenosis, where this emptiness empties itself of any substantialization and beingness. This *emptied emptiness* transcends all dualities and can only realize itself within them. Therefore, as in Mahāyāna, one must think from the *sive* or *soku*, from which all dualities have their origin and beginning. From the standpoint of emptiness (*śūnyatā*), all dualities (religion and science) are abolished. In order to enter the realm of *śūnyatā*, the discursive thinking of dualities must be negated. The *kōan* (公案)[40] serves in the meditation as the negation of the discursive thinking and leads to *satori* (悟り). From the standpoint of *śūnyatā* there is no difference between religion and science, subject and object, being and *nihilum*. Moreover, the speech and

---

38. Nishitani, *Religion and Nothingness*, 90.
39. Nishitani, *Religion and Nothingness*, 96–97.
40. Sekida, *Two Zen Classics*; Heine and Wright, *Kōan*.

thought of emptiness are also forbidden, since they are always discursive and unable to express the essence of *śūnyatā*. Based on the *Muchū Mondō* (夢中問答, Questions and answers in a dream), Kokushi Musō says the following sentences:

> Hills and rivers, the earth, plants and trees, tiles and stones, all of these are the self's own original part.
> It is not that the field of that original part lies in body-and-mind, or that it lies outside body-and-mind, or that body-and-mind are precisely the place of the original part, or that the original part is sentient or non-sentient, or that it is the wisdom of Buddhas and saints. Out of the realm of the original part have arisen all things: from the wisdom of Buddhas and saints to the body-and-mind of every sentient being, and all lands and worlds.[41]

Nishitani asks at the end of the seventh section of the third chapter, "Nihilism and *Sūnyatā*," what is the origin from which all things arise? Where is the plant plant, the stone stone and at the same time the self radically itself? In other words, where is the emptiness really empty?

3.3 Self-Nature (*Jishō*) and Non-Self-Nature (*Mu-Kishō*)

Aristotle defined a thing by using the substance-accident category. Substance refers to the unchanging nature of a thing. By substance is meant that it lies unchangeably and eternally at the bottom of a thing and denotes the self-identity of it. Even if the accidents are constantly changing, the substance remains the same. The concept of subject is closely linked to the concept of substance. The subject is that which cannot be objectified and which underlies all human thought and action. However, the true being-in-itself of a thing cannot be described using the categories of substance and subject. Rather, from the standpoint of emptiness, both are called into question. When the kenotic turn from *nihilum* to the field of emptiness is accomplished, the subject-object duality is transcended and the awareness of the true suchness of all things occurs:

> The mode of being of things when they are what they are in themselves, on their own home-ground, cut off from the sort of mode of being reflected in the subject-object relation, cannot be substantial, much less subjective.[42]

41. Nishitani, *Religion and Nothingness*, 108.
42. Nishitani, *Religion and Nothingness*, 112.

Now the following question arises: What is the true self-being of all things where they are on their home ground? This question is answered by Nishitani in sections 9 and 10 of chapter 3 using a practical example:

> Let us say a child is making a fire in the yard. There *is* a fire out there.[43]

The category of substance describes the actuality or self-identity of the fire. The fire is understood as that through which it becomes fire in the first place. The specific properties, the power, and the effectiveness of the burning describe the substance of fire. Therefore, the substance is nothing other than the form (εἶδος) of the fire, through which fire is distinguished from others and shows the specific property of burning. Fire can also be viewed scientifically or by the means of formal logic (*genus proximum* and *differentia specifica*), which describes the fire from the standpoint of the logos. But then the true being of fire is lost. It was analyzed by using the substance-accident category and by using the means of formal logic, whereby fire was objectified and lost its essence. The standpoint of logos is the standpoint of the subject-object duality and cannot describe the true self-being of fire. This is a different level, which describes the true mode of being of fire, that is, where the "thing is original and stands on itself, where it is at home in its selfhood." In section 10, Nishitani writes:

> "Fire does not burn fire," "Water does not wash water," "The eye does not see the eye."[44]

How should these Buddhist sayings be understood? How can they shed light on the true being-in-itself and the true self-identity of all things?

> But this is not the self-identity of fire as a "substance" viewed from a standpoint at which we view fire as an object. It is rather the self-identity of fire as fire in itself, on its own home-ground: the self-identity of fire to fire itself.[45]

In this quote it is clear that the Buddhist idioms express the true self-identity and have left the standpoint of substance. Now Nishitani has entered the field of emptiness. But what does true self-identity mean?

In the Buddhist saying "the fire does not burn fire," two dimensions must be distinguished from each other, which express the true self-identity:

43. Nishitani, *Religion and Nothingness*, 113; emphasis in original.
44. Nishitani, *Religion and Nothingness*, 116.
45. Nishitani, *Religion and Nothingness*, 116.

On the one hand, the sentence says that there is a fire (existence). On the other hand, the sentence states that fire can only exist in its selfhood and can be itself if it does not burn itself (nonexistence). Therefore, the fire must negate and empty itself. These two dimensions of burning and non-burning, affirmation and negation, constitute the true self-identity of fire. Act and non-act, burning and non-burning make up the mode of being a fire in its self-identity:

> That a fire has been kindled and is burned brightly means that the fire does not burn itself, that it insists on being itself and existing as what it is. In this facto fire's not burning itself, therefore, the essential being and actual being of fire are one. These words express the self-identity of fire, the self-identity of fire in itself on its own home-ground. They point directly to the "selfness" of fire.[46]

Now Nishitani has discovered the origin from which all things arise. The true place of being-in-itself is the place of true self-identity in which act and non-act are one. The essence consists in the self-identity of act and non-act, that is, fire is fire precisely if it does not burn itself when it burns. The self-identity of burning and non-burning constitutes the true essence of fire, not only in relation to us but also in relation to the fire itself. This means that on the field of self-identity the subject-object duality is transcended. At this point, self-nature and non-self-nature are just other terms for act and non-act, which characterize the being-in-itself of fire and its true self-identity. Both—self-nature (*jishō* 自性) and non-self-nature (*mujishō* 無自性)—thus express the *true self-identity* of fire:

> For this reason, we have to admit that even the self-identity of a fire as the fire it is, is unthinkable without its non-combustion. Self-nature is such as it is only as the self-nature of *non*-self-nature. The true self-identity of fire does not emerge from the self-identity it enjoys in combustion as a "substance" or a "self-nature," but only from the absolute negation of that self-identity, from its non-combustion.[47]

The true self-identity of the fire is the unity of burning and non-burning. Both dimensions—act and non-act—characterize the nature of fire. There can be no burning without non-burning and no non-burning without

---

46. Nishitani, *Religion and Nothingness*, 116.
47. Nishitani, *Religion and Nothingness*, 117–18; emphasis in original.

burning. Both dimensions imply each other and constitute the being-in-itself or the true self-identity of fire.

These ideas can also be transferred to the other two Buddhist idioms. In general, this means: true self-identity consists in the unity of identity (self-nature) and negation (non-self-nature), being and nonbeing. Therefore, fire is fire if and only if it is not fire; it is not fire if and only if it is fire. Now the *field of emptiness* has been reached:

> This absolutely surpassing field is none other than the field of *śūnyatā* spoken of earlier as the absolute near side.[48]

This is the place where "all things come and practice the self and confirm it or that mountains, rivers, the earth, plants and trees, bricks and stones are the very own of the self." In this way Nishitani transcends the *nihilum* towards the field of emptiness and practices a first kenosis. However, this is not enough, because the emptiness itself has to be emptied itself in a second kenosis. Then the true self-identity of emptiness can appear.

CONCLUSION: THE KENOSIS OF KENOSIS

If we now look at the double kenosis as it was worked out in relation to Cusanus and Nishitani, we can see similarities between them, but also differences that can be traced back to their cultural and religious backgrounds (Christianity and Zen Buddhism).

Similarities can be seen in particular in the fact that in both there is a first and a second kenosis: in Cusanus, this is the incarnation and resurrection of Jesus Christ; in Nishitani, this is the kenosis from nihilum to emptiness, and the emptying of emptiness itself. This kenosis must be followed by the kenosis of people: in Christianity, people must try to become like Jesus and walk on the path of virtue so that they are confirmed in Jesus having freed them from their sins and having justified them. In Zen Buddhism, humans must free themselves from their ego and countless attachments in order to realize the true self (emptiness of emptiness).

However, there are also differences between Cusanus and Nishitani that show their different points of view, i.e., mathematics and religion: if Cusanus creates a mathematical image of God, Nishitani creates an existential-religious image of God. According to Cusanus, Jesus Christ denotes an empty being (ontology), that is, a divine being that empties and negates

---

48. Nishitani, *Religion and Nothingness*, 118.

itself, then in Nishitani the emptiness itself transcends the duality of being and nothingness. Thus, Nishitani formulates a philosophy of emptiness that empties and negates itself.

In summary, Nishitani's philosophy of kenosis transcends that of Cusanus towards the field of emptiness. In doing so, Nishitani himself practices a kenosis *of* kenosis, that is, a kenosis that still negates and empties itself. Therefore, this can also be called an *absolute kenosis*.—Finally, I would like to ask what does it mean for the intercultural dialogue between Western and Eastern thinking, and how can it help us today to transcend the contemporary crises of the world?

First, an intercultural dialogue can be successful only if the cultures meet in an open conversation. The prerequisite for this is that they free themselves from any dogmatic point of view and become empty. This is the first kenosis as a prerequisite for the encounter with the other. This is followed by the second kenosis, which consists in the fact that in the dialogue both reach a point of view that transcends their particular cultures towards a *world philosophy*.

Second, the chapter showed that the incarnation of Jesus Christ and the arising of the *nihilum* in modernity are signs of the negation of humanity. Cusanus showed that humans are full of sins and evil and turned themselves away from God. Nishitani described the European nihilism where humans are slaves of technology and stand at the abyss of existence. This is also the description of the contemporary crises, like the Corona virus, the wars between Ukraine and Russia, Israel and Gaza, climate crises, and so on. In theological words: humans lost their paradise, which was the first kenosis. To be freed from their negation and inhumanity, humans have to negate themselves a second time. They have to practice a second kenosis to negate the inhumanity of today and to find their true self-identity. This is not an act of self-power (*jiriki*, 自力) but of the grace of God or the Other-power (*tariki*, 他力). Only then the human beings can find and realize *true freedom*. Tanabe writes in his *Philosophy as Metanoetics*:

> Without the aid of this Other-power, the human freedom of self-power is closed off to us. . . . The realization of human freedom in self-power becomes possible only through the assistance of Other-power.[49]

---

49. Tanabe, *Philosophy as Metanoetics*, 184.

BIBLIOGRAPHY

Beierwaltes, Werner. *Der verborgene Gott: Cusanus und Dionysius*. 2nd ed. Trierer Cusanus Lecture 4. Trier: Paulinus, 2008.

Bormann, Karl. *Nikolaus von Kues: "Der Mensch als zweiter Gott."* Trierer Cusanus Lecture 5. Trier: Paulinus, 1999.

Brösch, Marco, et al., eds. *Handbuch Nikolaus von Kues: Leben und Werk*. Darmstadt: Wissenschaftliche Buchgesellschaft, 2014.

Davis, Bret W. "Nishitani After Nietzsche: From the Death of God to the Great Death of the Will." In *Japanese and Continental Philosophy: Conversations with the Kyoto School*, edited by Bret W. Davis et al., 82–101. Studies in Continental Thought. Bloomington: Indiana University Press, 2011.

Deguchi, Yasuo. "Nishitani on Emptiness and Nothingness." In *Nothingness in Asian Philosophy*, edited by JeeLoo Liu and Douglas L. Berger, 300–325. London: Routledge, 2014.

Flasch, Kurt. *Nicolaus Cusanus*. Munich: Beck, 2001.

———. *Nikolaus von Kues: Geschichte einer Entwicklung, Vorlesungen zur Einführung in seine Philosophie*. Frankfurt am Main: Klostermann, 2001.

Hantke, Myriam-Sonja. *F. W. J. Schellings Identitätsphilosophie im Horizont der Kyōto-Schule*. Munich: Iudicium, 2005.

———. *Mística en la Filosofía Alemana y Japonesa*. Translated by Zaida Olvera. Nagoya: Chisokudō, 2009.

———. *Mystik im Deutschen Idealismus und in der Japanischen Philosophie: Schelling, Hegel, Nishitani*. Nordhausen: Traugott Bautz, 2009.

———. *Das Nicht-Andere: Zur Religionsphilosophie von Nikolaus von Kues, G. W. F. Hegel und der Kyôto-Schule*. Studien zur Weltgeschichte des Denkens Denktraditionen—neu entdeckt 6. Münster: LIT, 2022.

———. *Die Poesie der All-Einheit bei Friedrich Hölderlin und Nishida Kitaro*. Weltphilosophien im Gespräch 3. Nordhausen: Traugott Bautz, 2009.

Haubst, Rudolf. *Das Bild des Einen und Dreieinen Gottes in der Welt nach Nikolaus von Kues*. Trierer Theologische Studien 4. Trier: Paulinus, 1952.

———. *Die Christologie des Nikolaus von Kues*. Freiburg: Herder, 1956.

Heine, Steven, and Dale S. Wright, eds. *The Kōan: Texts and Contexts in Zen Buddhism*. New York: Oxford University Press, 2000.

Hopkins, Jasper. *Nicholas of Cusa on Learned Ignorance: A Translation and an Appraisal of "De Docta Ignorantia."* 2nd ed. Minneapolis: Banning, 1985.

Jones, David. "Empty Soul, Empty World: Nietzsche and Nishitani." In *Japanese and Continental Philosophy: Conversations with the Kyoto School*, edited by Bret W. Davis et al., 102–19. Studies in Continental Thought. Bloomington: Indiana University Press, 2011.

Kitamori, Kazoh. *Theologie des Schmerzes Gottes*. Theologie der Ökumene 11. Göttingen: Vandenhoeck & Ruprecht, 1972.

Kruger, Matthew C. *The Gospel and Nothingness*. Nagoya: Chisokudo, 2019.

Kues, Nikolaus von. *Apologia Doctae Ignorantiae*. HAA 2. Hamburg: Meiner, 1932.

———. *Die belehrte Unwissenheit (De Docta Ignorantia)*. Edited by H. G. Senger. 3 vols. 4th ed. Hamburg: Meiner, 1994.

———. *Dialogus de Deo Abscondito*. HAA 4. Hamburg: Meiner, 1959.

———. *Der Friede im Glauben (De Pace Fidei)*. Translated by Rudolf Haubst. 3rd ed. Trier: Paulinus, 2003.

———. *Mutmaßungen (De Coniecturis)*. Edited by Josef Koch and Winfried Happ. 2nd ed. Hamburg: Meiner, 1988.

———. *De Non Aliud (Nichts Anderes)*. Edited by Klaus Reinhardt et al. Münster: Aschendorff, 2011.

———. *Philosophisch-theologische Schriften*. Edited by Leo Gabriel. Translated by Dietland Dupre and Wilhelm Dupre. 3 vols. Freiburg im Breisgau: Herder, 1964–76.

———. *Das Sehen Gottes (De Visione Dei)*. Translated by Helmut Pfeiffer. 3rd ed. Trier: Paulinus, 2007.

———. *Über den Beryll (De Beryllo)*. Edited by Karl Bormann. 3rd ed. Hamburg: Meiner, 1987.

Nishitani, Keiji. 西谷啓治著作集 [*Chosakushū*, Collected works]. 26 vols. Tokyo: Sōbunsha, 1986–95.

———. "Emptiness and Sameness." *Modern Japanese Aesthetics: A Reader*, edited by Michele Marra, 179–217. Honolulu: University of Hawaii Press, 1999.

———. "Mein philosophischer Ausgangspunkt." Translated by R. Elberfeld. *Zeitschrift für philosophische Forschung* 46 (1992) 545–56.

———. *Nishida Kitarō*. Translated by Yamamoto Seisaku and James W. Heisig. Introduction by D. S. Clarke Jr. Nanzan Studies in Religion and Culture. Berkeley: University of California Press, 1991.

———. "Ontology and Utterance." *Philosophy East and West* 31 (1981) 29–43.

———. *Religion and Nothingness*. Translated by Jan van Bragt. Nanzan Studies in Religion and Culture. Berkeley: University of California Press, 1982.

———. *Was ist Religion?* Translated by D. Fischer-Barnicol. 2nd ed. Frankfurt am Main: Insel, 1986.

Sekida, Katsuki, ed. and trans. *Two Zen Classics: Mumonkan and Hekiganroku*. Edited by A. V. Grimstone. 3rd ed. New York: Weatherhill, 1996.

Stallmach, Josef. *Ineinsfall der Gegensätze und Weisheit des Nichtwissens: Grundzüge der Philosophie des Nikolaus von Kues*. Münster: Aschendorff, 1989.

———. "Das 'Nichtandere' als Begriff des Absoluten: Zur Auswertung der mystischen Theologie des Pseudo-Dionysius durch Cusanus." In *Universitas, Festschrift für Bischof Dr. A. Stohr*, edited by Ludwig Lenhart, 1:329–35. Mainz: Matthias Grünewald, 1996.

Tanabe, Hajime. *Philosophy as Metanoetics*. Translated by Yoshinori Takeuchi. Nanzan Studies in Religion and Culture. Berkeley: University of California Press, 1986.

Weber-Brosamer, Bernhard, and Dieter M. Back, eds. *Die Philosophie der Leere: Nāgārjunas Mūlamadhyamaka-Kārikās*. Beitrage zur Indologie. Wiesbaden: Harrassowitz, 1997.

Williams, David T. *Kenōsis of God. The Self-Limitation of God: Father, Son, and Holy Spirit*. New York: iUniverse, 2009.

Yamaki, Kazuhiko. "Das elliptische Denken des Cusanus: Zur Cusanus-Rezeption in Japan." *Mittelalter* 19 (2014) 146–66.

Yamaki, Kazuhiko. *Anregung und Übung: Zur Laienphilosophie des Nikolaus von Kues*. Texte und Studien zur europäischen Geistesgeschichte 15. Münster: Aschendorff, 2017.

8

Kenosis, Dynamic *Śūnyatā*, and Weak Thought
Abe Masao and Gianni Vattimo

THORSTEN BOTZ-BORNSTEIN

INTRODUCTION

ABE MASAO (1915–2006) WAS one of the leading exponents of Japanese Buddhism in Japan as well as for Western audiences. In this chapter, I want to compare his thoughts on the Christian concept of the divine kenosis with those of the Italian philosopher Gianni Vattimo (1936–2023) on the same subject. Vattimo's idea that "true Christianity must be nonreligious" will be proven compatible with elements of Abe's interpretation of kenosis. Parallels between Abe's and Vattimo's thought will be demonstrated with regard to themes current in East-West comparative philosophy: reality and emptiness, the overcoming of metaphysics, the position of the self, the human and the divine, and the relationship between science and religion. Finally, Abe's interpretation of *śūnyatā* will be presented as a form of "weak thought."

One of the purposes of this chapter is to produce a genuinely philosophical discourse on Abe's *śūnyatā* discussion that is not tainted by certain theological themes. In spite of its intellectual wealth and sophistication, a more conceptual East-West *philosophical* discussion of the kenosis-*śūnyatā* problem has never been produced.[1] Instead, the Western responses to Japanese kenoticism have almost exclusively been formulated by Western *theologians*, most of whom have attempted to reintegrate the kenosis theme into the ecclesial context of Phil 2. Many were trying to re-root kenosis in the sacramental basis of the church or in the liturgical, biblical, and patristic dimensions of Christianity. A repeated reproach is therefore that Abe reinterprets Christianity in terms of his own Buddhist categories. Many Christian and Jewish theologians have taken issue at Abe's way of approaching kenosis through his anti-theistic skepticism or could not accept his *philosophical* idea to present "a revolutionary reinterpretation of the concept of God in Christianity and the concept of emptiness in Buddhism."[2] The theology bias applies for criticism as well as for approval.[3] Given its rootedness in *theological* discussions, most criticism of the kenosis-*śūnyatā* parallelism is determined not so much by the potentials and limits of comparative *philosophy*, but by the potentials and limits of *interreligious* communication. Continental philosophy, in spite of the importance it has had for the Kyoto School in general, is clearly underrepresented. Steve Odin's pages on the kenosis-*śūnyatā* theme and pragmatism count among the few exceptions.[4]

The main purpose of the present comparative study is thus to elucidate aspects of kenosis and *śūnyatā* that could perhaps not have been found otherwise. For example, at first sight, the idea to compare kenosis and *śūnyatā* is surprising because kenosis is a process while *śūnyatā*, in most cases, is described as a state. Abe's strategy is to see *śūnyatā* precisely as a process: constantly in need of being emptied of its substance in order to avoid reification, *śūnyatā* is "self-emptying" and not simply "emptiness" (which is why it should not be identified with God). Also Vattimo's kenosis-inspired

1. Charles Jones has indicated further limitations in a more recent article. According to him, the problem is that each side seems to have extracted knowledge about the other religion from a very limited number of texts. Further, Jones finds that Buddhist-Christian dialogue has long since moved on, focusing "more on social and ethical issues than on philosophy" (Jones mentions the revival of the Buddhist-Christian Theological Encounters organized by Donald Mitchell in the late 1990s) (Jones, "Emptiness, Kenosis, History," 130).

2. Abe, "Kenotic God and Dynamic *Śūnyatā*," 4.

3. Approval has been looked for in representatives of "new-style" kenotic Christology (developed by J. Robinson and J. Macquarrie) who see kenosis as "self-fulfilling emptying" and the fullest expression of love because "kenosis is plerosis" (Odin, "Critique of '*Kenōsis/Śūnyatā*' Motif," 75).

4. Odin, "Critique of '*Kenōsis/Śūnyatā*' Motif."

philosophy sees Christian religion not as a reified metaphysical statement but as a call to practice, which is "the truth of love and charity."[5] This overlaps with Abe's idea that "just like *śūnyatā* must empty itself and turn itself into vow, it must empty even vow and turn itself into act or deed, which is traditionally called *carita* or *carya*"[6] and that when "the 'vow' empties itself, it turns into the 'act' of saving self and others."[7] Vattimo's philosophy of "weak thought" coincides here with Abe's views on Zen-Buddhism because both see emptiness not as merely nihilistic but as dynamic.

A further purpose of this chapter is to introduce Vattimo's thought into the area of comparative philosophy. Vattimo has never had much intercultural ambition and has never addressed—as far as I can see—philosophical problems pertaining to non-Western cultures. On the other hand, when Vattimo says that he defines himself "as Christian because I believe that Christianity is more 'true' than all the other religions precisely on account of the fact that there is a sense in which *it is not a religion*," he naturally invites comparisons with Buddhism, because controversies over its status as a religion have accompanied Buddhism for centuries.[8]

Vattimo is a specialist of hermeneutic philosophy, which he developed into a personal philosophical system called *weak thought*. Weak thought made its first appearance in 1983 and can be seen as an Italian version of poststructuralism. It defines itself in opposition to diverse philosophies of the nineteenth and twentieth centuries: Hegelian dialectics, Marxism, phenomenology, psychoanalysis, and structuralism. Weak thought refrains from absolute truths and prefers to concentrate on the frail, the impermanent, and the historical element in human existence. It is also meant as a key notion for the democratization of society. What it shares with other postmodern philosophies is the intention to deconstruct "strong thought" manifest in the form of progressivist or universalist conceptions of truth, history, fixed identities as well as traditions and monotheistic theologies. Though it is critical of systematic thinking and deductive cogency, weak thought has managed, during all stages of its development, to stay away from the negative nihilism typical for other postmodern theories.

Abe was a professor of philosophy and religious studies and a practicing Buddhist linked to the Kyoto School. Like few others, he has emphasized

---

5. Abe, "Kenotic God and Dynamic *Śūnyatā*," 51.
6. Abe, "Kenotic God and Dynamic *Śūnyatā*," 58.
7. Abe, "Will, *Śūnyatā*, and History," 302.
8. Vattimo and Girard, *Christianity, Truth, Weakening Faith*, 52; emphasis in original.

the necessity of interreligious dialogue. Together with Suzuki Daisetz, he has probably been the main representative of Zen Buddhism in the West.

1. COMPARING *ŚŪNYATĀ* AND KENOSIS

The *śūnyatā*-kenosis exchange is one of the most original Buddhist-Christian dialogues in philosophy of religion in the twentieth century and has built a unique bridge between the two religions. The idea of a strong and strengthening God typical for monotheistic religions (sometimes leading to fundamentalism) can appear as incompatible with the Buddhist prerogative of impermanence and its insistence on the relative, relational, non-substantial, and changeable character of everything. However, the kenosis theme allows Christianity to appear in another light. According to Vattimo, a thinking based on kenosis opposes physico-mechanical visions of the world as well as authoritarian metaphysical structures. Being less anthropocentric, it also criticizes the view that humans are made in the image of God and tends to insist on the interrelatedness of things. The latter three points make a kenosis-based philosophy compatible with some central Buddhist views.

Based on the above parallels, in Japan, kenosis has generated a rich discourse on Buddhist-Christian parallels showing that both Buddhism and Christianity can see self-emptying as an ideal of human perfection. "Japanese kenoticism"[9] is a sophisticated project that transcends previous schools of German, British, or Russian kenoticism.[10] The kenosis-*śūnyatā* parallel has been addressed by Kyoto School philosophers Nishida Kitaro and Nishitani Keiji, as well as many other Japanese thinkers. Nishitani wrote that "the Buddhist way of life as well as its way of thought are permeated with kenosis and ekkenosis."[11] The late 1980s and 1990s saw the production of an exceptionally extensive amount of literature on the parallels between Christian kenosis and Buddhist *śūnyatā*. The discussion was sparked by Abe's paper "Kenotic God and Dynamic *Śūnyatā*" delivered at the "East-West Religions in Encounter" conference in Honolulu in 1984. The paper will be central to the present chapter. It inspired three volumes of responses by Western (Christian and Jewish) theologians as well as many other

---

9. Odin, "Critique of '*Kenōsis/Śūnyatā*' Motif."
10. See Cabanne, "Beyond Kenosis," 102.
11. Nishitani, *Religion and Nothingness*, 288n4.

responses by Western theologians.[12] The process theologian John B. Cobb in particular was intrigued by parallels between the Japanese discussion of kenosis and his own work.

Vattimo uses kenosis as the hermeneutic key to the interpretation of Christian religion. More precisely, kenosis refers to a process he calls *secularization*: when strong structures such as the essence and the fulfilment of the Christian message are weakened, we find a truth that cannot be obtained without the abasement, humiliation, and weakening of God. Vattimo translates kenosis as "weakening" and claims that secularization represents an integral part of the Christian program because weak ontology is the real heir of the Christian tradition: "Voltaire was a good Christian precisely because he demanded freedom against authoritarianism. . . . In this way perhaps true Christianity must be nonreligious."[13] This means that modernity does not lead to nihilism in the way it was thought by Nietzsche and Heidegger, but rather to a nonreligious or secular form of Christianity.

Vattimo's strategy of open-endedness is unusual in a Christian context if one considers that normally, the Christian view of history is determined by eschatology or apocalypticism. Abe himself highlights this difference and insists that this aspect of Christianity remains incompatible with the philosophy of *śūnyatā*: "Telos in the *śūnyatā*-oriented view of history is not a definitive, closed end, like the Christian notion of the Kingdom of God coming through the Last Judgment at the end of history, but a boundlessly open end without a fixed purpose."[14]

In his writings on the *śūnyatā*-kenosis theme Abe attempts to import elements of radical and existential skepticism into Christian religion, which is precisely the strategy of weak thought. Both Abe and Vattimo think that when existence is questioned in terms of nothingness, a real religious feeling is bound to emerge. Skepticism discards all false substances and universals without discarding religion as such. This contradicts basic Christian presuppositions, which, according to Coakley, since the fourth or fifth century take "Christ's substantial pre-existence and essential divinity for granted."[15]

---

12. Cobb and Ives, *Emptying God*; Corless and Knitter, *Buddhist Emptiness and Christian Trinity*; Ives, *Divine Emptiness and Historical Fullness*.

13. Vattimo, "Toward a Nonreligious Christianity," 36–37.

14. Abe, "Will, *Śūnyatā*, and History," 302.

15. Coakley, *Powers and Submissions*, 12.

2. REALITY AND EMPTINESS

Both Abe and Vattimo design a religious attitude based on negativity without falling into the trap of anti-religion. This negativity has startled many theologians, as Vattimo points out himself:

> Christian interlocutors, and not just the most orthodox but also those who do not seem very orthodox but nonetheless incline towards a tragic or apocalyptic Christianity, always complain that in the secularized or weak conception of Christianity the harshness, severity and rigor characteristic of divine justice are lost, and with them the meaning of sin, the actuality of evil, and as a consequence even the necessity of redemption.[16]

Jürgen Moltmann reproaches Abe (and Buddhism in general) for the lack of concreteness and actuality when it comes to evil: "Buddhism has indeed cosmically interpreted the problem of evil with the help of the term karma, but with that, it has too quickly disregarded the moral and political dimensions of evil."[17] Finally, Hans Küng regrets that Abe sees both *śūnyatā* and kenosis in purely negative terms, never spelling out a positive quality that could be obtained after undergoing the process of kenosis or *śūnyatā*.

When critics of Vattimo's weak religion miss a depiction of evil in its "actuality," they do indeed recognize an important quality of weak thought. Vattimo believes that only when we deconstruct the "objective truth" of God, can we grasp the "redemptive meaning of the Christian message."[18] This means that neither God nor evil reside in the realm of the necessary, the actual, or the positive. Vattimo refers to Heidegger's "rhetorical conception of truth" but he could as well speak of a rhetorical concept of God. Here "Being experiences the fullness of its decline (as Heidegger understands it when he says that the Western world is the land of the crepuscule of being), fully living its weakness."[19]

Vattimo does not refer to Eastern religions to support his thesis about the weakening of the real. First, nihilism, the dissolution of all ultimate foundations, is for him part of the history of philosophy and Western culture formulated by Hegel, Marx, Nietzsche, and Heidegger.[20] Second,

---

16. Vattimo, *After Christianity*, 87–88.
17. Moltmann, "God Is Unselfish Love," 117.
18. Vattimo, *After Christianity*, 87–88.
19. Vattimo, "Dialectics, Difference, Weak Thought," 50.
20. See Vattimo, "Nihilism as Emancipation," 20.

Christianity remains for Vattimo a ne plus ultra of *Western* civilization, as Zabala points out: "Vattimo thinks it is not possible to have a 'non-Christian philosophy' because philosophy is a historical product of our Western culture and civilization."[21] Instead of referring to Eastern weak definitions of Being and reality (certain approaches towards nothingness, for example), Vattimo refers to the increasing "virtualization" of reality (in its broadest sense) as the typically "Western" destiny. For him, recent events within industrialized capitalist countries, most notably the invention of virtual reality, prove that "the Christian West" is moving away from a centered, actual reality, which means that it goes the way it was bound to go from its kenotic beginning. While the West is losing the will to demonstrate a stable sense of reality and nihilism leads to the "dissolution of the 'principle of reality,'"[22] the internet provides a suitable mode of Being that remains removed from both metaphysical realism and Platonic essentialism. As weak thought avoids primary, "metaphysical" ways of being that remain dependent on a Cartesian ego cogito[23] or on concepts and propositions valid only because they correspond with an independent objective reality "out there," virtual reality represents the most suitable alternative:

> If the West seeks its own identity, it must principally reckon with the phenomena indicated above, namely a Weberian capitalist rationalization plus the world of information and of proliferating interpretations without a center, which tends to weaken the sense of the terms being and reality. . . . Not only is the West today only definable as a unified entity as secularized Christianity, but also, Christianity today rediscovers itself authentically only if it identifies itself as Western. In other and more provocative words: I mean that today the West, understood as the land of the sunset and of weakening, is Christianity's truth.[24]

The Christian kenotic heritage will lead to secularization in the sense of a weakening of reality. The curious interlinking of secularization, nihilism, and virtual reality—all inscribed in a genuine "Christian destiny"—is what makes Vattimo's weak thought unique. It is also the reason Vattimo's antimetaphysical philosophy indicating the weakening of reality is opposed to classic interpretations of kenosis.

21. Zabala, *Weakening Philosophy*, 22–23.
22. Vattimo, *Beyond Interpretation*, 26.
23. See Heidegger, "Überwindung der Metaphysik," 70.
24. Vattimo, *Belief*, 79.

It goes without saying that Vattimo's "emancipation based on oscillation, plurality and, ultimately, the erosion of the very 'principle of reality'" is not the favored option of Christian theologians when attempting to formulate a faith based on kenosis.[25] Most Christian theologians prefer to see kenosis in terms of a *very strong* form of reality, often by formulating it in terms of the self-realization of Christ. Some refer to verses 9–11 of the Pauline hymn (Phil 2), which emphasizes God's resurrection. This further clarifies the contrast with Vattimo because any "actuality" is the contrary of virtual reality. Moltmann insists that the emptying of God is nothing but the self-realization of the Son: "But because the *emptying of himself* to the point of death on the cross happens in obedience to God, one must say at the same time that the *self-realization* of the son of God is also accomplished in it. It is an active kenosis of the divine which only the son can accomplish."[26]

A few words need to be said in order to avoid the impression that the "Eastern" view (together with Vattimo's embrace of virtual reality) is fleeing reality and merely settling in an "unreal" sphere of the virtual. As will become clear below, the Zen-Buddhist view of reality—to which Abe adheres—is nonempirical, but not in the sense that it would see reality as an idealized dream world. On the contrary, the Zen-Buddhist view is *realistic* because it aims at "knowing facts as they are" by experiencing facts in a "pure" fashion and in their most original form.[27] The only difference with conventional reality is that their reality is not the reality of subjective certitudes or metaphysical universals: it is neither subjective in the Cartesian sense nor an objectified reality (consciousness). Abe holds that "consciousness is the sole reality [and] not objectified consciousness."[28] We will return to this point later.

3. THE OVERCOMING OF METAPHYSICS

Vattimo's approach depends on an ironical construction of what he calls "half belief." The half believer is religious, but just *because* he is religious he refrains from transferring limited notions of scientific truth to the realms of religion, ethics, and philosophy. In this sense, the "half believer"

---

25. Vattimo, *Transparent Society*, 7.
26. Moltmann, "God Is Unselfish Love," 118; emphasis in original.
27. Nishitani, *Nishida Kitarō*, 98.
28. Abe, "Nishida's Philosophy of Place," 356.

participates in the postmodern project of overcoming metaphysics. Vattimo's weak theology is supposed to weaken dogmatic as well as "religio-scientific" tendencies, which occur primarily when "strong" beliefs are expressed in "scientific" and metaphysical terms. Vattimo bases his criticism of Christian theology on Heidegger's interpretation of metaphysics as the objective truth of Being from which arose a dogmatic moral teaching.[29] Also John Caputo defines weak theology as "a weakening of the militant dogmatic tendencies of the confessional theologies, which in modernity fused in a lethal way with the Cartesian paradigm of certitude."[30]

Both *śūnyatā* and kenosis run counter to traditional Western metaphysical frameworks. In general, the ambitions of weak theology—just like those of pragmatism—consist in the overcoming of metaphysical distinctions that are both Christian-theological and Platonic-philosophical, and in finding an "intermediary way between entrusting oneself to a divine substitute and entrusting oneself to individual preferences."[31] In this sense, kenosis is opposed to traditions that think of reality in terms of being, such as the Aristotelian logic of predication. This is also the reason Christian theology has always had difficulty integrating the notion of kenosis *philosophically* "insofar as Christian theology was committed to a static Greek metaphysics of unchanging being or eternal substance."[32]

3.1. *Verwindung*

Both Vattimo and the Kyoto School philosophers attempt to reformulate kenosis in terms of a nonsubstantialist metaphysics.[33] Vattimo divides for

---

29. See Vattimo, *After Christianity*, 49.
30. Caputo, "Spectral Hermeneutics," 73.
31. Zabala, *Weakening Philosophy*, 3.
32. Odin, "Critique of '*Kenōsis/Śūnyatā*' Motif," 82.

33. Abe affirms that *śūnyatā* is fundamentally "not a metaphysical but a religious and soteriological notion" (*Buddhism and Interfaith Dialogue*, 54). However, paradoxically, just because of its anti-metaphysical input as well as the radical thoughts about the existence of reality linked to the topic, the *śūnyatā* discussion is not only related to existential philosophy (which bears a natural link with religion) but is also metaphysical (or anti-metaphysical) by definition. In the words of Chappell, Abe uses *śūnyatā* "as a metaphysical description of reality" ("Introduction," 13) and deconstructs this description. David Dilworth's statement that "the Christian perspective is "noumenal in ontological focus" does not make the Christian perspective incompatible with the Kyoto School approach. Dilworth finds that the latter is determined by "the existential signification of Buddhist discourse" while the Christian side gives priority to metaphysics ("Nishida's Critique,"

this purpose weak thought into two branches, which he calls the right-wing and the left-wing branch, each of which is related to the Heideggerian distinction between *Überwindung* (overcoming) and the more complex *Verwindung*. The latter word is used rather sparingly by Heidegger,[34] but it has been important for Vattimo's early philosophical development.[35] As opposed to the more straightforward *Überwindung* (overcoming), *Verwindung* is a sort of improper, twisted, distorted, and ironical kind of overcoming. For Vattimo it represents the "declination of difference into weak thought."[36] The right-wing interpretation demands "the return of Being by overcoming (*Überwindung*) metaphysics as an effort while the left-wing interpretation demands a 'resigning' (*Verwindung*) to the reading of the history of Being as an interminable weakening of Being."[37] Thus, *Verwindung* marks for Vattimo "the attitude which characterizes post-metaphysical thought in relation to the tradition handed down by metaphysics."[38] It is worthwhile to explain the scope of the *Verwindung* in more precise terms, especially since the "left-wing" position bears a conceptual link with the Buddhist resignation.

First of all, *Verwindung* must be reflected against another Heideggerian term, that of *herausdrehen* (to twist out of, to twist free of). Heidegger intended to overcome Platonism not by means of its simple "overturning" (*herumdrehen*), but by what he called a "twisting out" (*Herausdrehen*) of philosophy from a movement that he saw as an endless chain of overturnings of Platonism. In his first volume on Nietzsche he writes:

> What happens when the true world is expunged? Does the apparent world still remain? No. For the apparent world can be what it is only as a counterpart of the true: if the true world collapses, so must the world of appearances. Only then is Platonism overcome, which is to say, inverted in such a way that philosophical thinking twists free of it.[39]

---

45). The problem is rather that the Christian side is fixated on theological problems like resurrection, exaltation, etc.

34. It appears in one passage in "Spruch des Anaximander" (in *Holzwege*), in "Überwindung der Metaphysik" (in *Vorträge und Aufsätze*), and in *Identität und Differenz*.

35. See Vattimo, "*Verwindung*."

36. Vattimo, "Dialectics, Difference, Weak Thought," 45.

37. Zabala, *Weakening Philosophy*, 17.

38. Vattimo, "Dialectics, Difference, Weak Thought," 46.

39. Heidegger, *Nietzsche* (1979), 1:201. "Was geschieht, wenn die wahre Welt abgeschafft wird? Bleibt dann noch die scheinbare Welt? Nein. Denn die scheinbare Welt

Platonic realism produces a purely general view of the world dealing only with "essences" and abstractions, which Nietzsche wants to "overturn" by calling the sensible the real and the non-sensible unreal. According to Heidegger, the entire history of philosophy is the history of such overturnings. Hegel's metaphysics of certitude, for example, is generally said to have collapsed in the nineteenth century, but in reality the movements opposing Hegelianism are continuations of Hegel's philosophy.[40] Heidegger wants to abolish Platonism, but not in order to go for the other extreme, which would be scientific anthropology or (in the view of Nietzsche) "positivism," both of which remain restricted to the analysis of the concrete and individual. Instead, Heidegger's *Herausdrehen* of philosophy out of two extremes is supposed to result in a philosophical hermeneutics. The main characteristic of this hermeneutics is that it adheres neither to a generalist (Platonic) nor to an individualist (empirical) view, but strives for the simultaneous manipulation of the "individual" and the "general." This hermeneutics is directly related to the paradox of the hermeneutic circle, which Heidegger understands mainly as a methodological means of constantly holding back any final decision in favor of either a generalist or an individualist approach. Quite famously, Heidegger views the hermeneutic circle as a "positive possibility of understanding":

> But if interpretation must in any case already operate in that which is under-stood, and if it must draw its nurture from this, how is it to bring any scientific results to maturity without moving in a circle, especially if, moreover, the understanding which is presupposed still operates within our common information about man and the world?[41]

Heidegger's affirmation of the circle does not signify a resignation in the sense of an intellectual fatalism, which would be the belief that knowledge as such is impossible. The hermeneutic circle does not condemn us to

---

kann das, was es ist, nur sein als Gegenstück zur wahren. Wenn diese fällt, muß auch die scheinbare fallen. Erst dann ist der Platonismus überwunden, d.h. so umgedreht, daß das philosophische Denken aus ihm herausgedreht wird" (Heidegger, *Nietzsche* [1961], 1:233).

40. Heidegger, "Überwindung der Metaphysik," 72.

41. Heidegger, *Being and Time*, 195. "Wenn aber Auslegung sich je schon im Verstandenen bewegen und aus ihm her sich nähren muß, wie soll sie dann wissenschaftliche Resultaten zeitigen, ohne sich in einem Zirkel zu bewegen, zumal wenn das vorausgesetzte Verständnis überdies noch in der gemeinen Menschen und Weltkenntnis sich bewegt?" (Heidegger, *Sein und Zeit*, 152).

eternally stay in the sphere of "common knowledge of man and the world." It is the scientist (and perhaps the theologian) who sees the circle as a vitiosum that needs to be avoided. The person who simply "tolerates" (*duldet*) the circle has resigned from any possibility of positive understanding and develops an equally indifferent attitude toward everyday life.[42] Opposed to this, Heidegger asks for an active affirmation of the circle because it negates everyday life. It helps us *verwinden* the conventional character of Being (the "man" or the "durchschnittliche Seinsverständnis").

Here we can come back to Buddhism. The active and affirmative character of hermeneutics joins Abe's vision of *śūnyatā*, which represents for Abe, like for his teacher Hisamatsu, not a retreat or a simple resignation, but a positive (though *verwunden*) coming back into life:

> Sunyata should not be understood as a goal or end to be attained in Buddhist life, but as the ground and the point of departure from which Buddhist life and activity can properly begin. Sunyata as the goal or end of Buddhist life is Sunyata conceived outside one's self-existence, which is not true Sunyata. The true Sunyata is only realized in and through the self here and now and is always the ground or the point of departure for Buddhist life.[43]

In the words of Suzuki Daisetz, the absolute self should "not remain content with itself" but go out "to a world of multitudes."[44] Otherwise it is not free but becomes a slave of *saṅkhāra* (conditioned things).[45] For Suzuki, a higher field of consciousness can only be reached "by living it, seeing into its working, by actually experiencing the significance of life, or by tasting the value of living."[46] Buddha did not teach the religion of eternal death. Also Hisamatsu insists that Buddhism does not lead to a serene and self-enclosed *nirvāṇa* but that "true serenity is nothing objective; it is not merely being tranquil or not being disturbed. It is rather being what may be called the Fundamental Subject or Absolute."[47] A *Verwindung*-based hermeneutics follows similar lines.

---

42. I have explained Heidegger's concept of "overturning" in a more detailed fashion in Botz-Bornstein, *Philosophy of Lines*, 165–68.
43. Abe, "Kenotic God and Dynamic *Śūnyatā*," 33.
44. Suzuki, *Mysticism*, 47.
45. *Saṃskāra* in Sanskrit.
46. Suzuki, *Mysticism*, 47.
47. Hisamatsu, *Zen and Fine Arts*, 59.

3.2 "Credere di Credere"

Abe's negation of the subject, which leads to a pluralism of beings, can also be compared with Vattimo's paradoxical "credere di credere" (to believe to believe), through which Vattimo describes the attitude of an ego that has lost its own subjectivity. The person who does not believe but only "believes to believe" is a sort of nonego. The ego is deconstructed through a long chain of "believe to believe to believe . . ." coming close to a Pyrrhonian suspension of judgment (*epoché*). This process obviously has a parallel in Kyoto School Buddhism, which insists very much on the negation of the negation. Abe frequently refers in his article to the fact that in order to attain "true non-discriminative equality with others, even *anattā* [*anātman* (no self)] must be negated."[48] For Vattimo the "deep uncertainty of opinion"[49] flowing out of the "believe to believe" attitude, leads to a "nothingness" similar to the nothingness sought by Abe when referring to *śūnyatā*. The "belief" flowing out of a "believe to believe" can no longer be contrasted with enlightened reason. The same is true for Abe's Buddhist paradigm of simultaneously being and not being God. This is how both Abe and Vattimo deconstruct religious subjectivity without abandoning religious faith altogether. Vattimo's skeptical "believe to believe" is still produced by religious belief and is even supposed to maintain belief. Abe writes that "in the kenotic God who is *Nichts*, not only are modern human autonomous reason and rationalistic subjectivity overcome . . . but also the mystery of God is most profoundly perceived."[50] He concludes that the kenotic God goes "beyond atheism and theism,"[51] which expresses an attitude similar to Vattimo's "half belief." Those philosophies are not atheist or scientific critiques of religion but rather "half-theistic" ways of thinking God that are remarkable in a world in which Christianity seems to have failed to present a compelling alternative to scientism and nihilism.

3.3. The Self and Self-Centeredness

Vattimo also ties to *Verwindung* the term *pietà* (compassion) because compassion "may be another term which, along with *Andenken* and

48. Abe, "Rejoinder" (1990), 198.
49. Vattimo, *Belief*, 2.
50. Abe, "Kenotic God and Dynamic *Śūnyatā*," 26.
51. Abe, "Kenotic God and Dynamic *Śūnyatā*," 26.

Verwindung, could characterize the weak thought of postmetaphysics."[52] Since *pietà* "suggests primarily mortality, finitude and passing away," Vattimo describes it—in a quasi-Buddhist way—as "*the transcendental, or that which makes any experience of the world possible, [it] is nothing less than transcience [caducità]*."[53] Basing his thoughts on both Heidegger and Nietzsche's "death of God" philosophy, Vattimo concludes that "Being means to recall such transitoriness [*caducità*]."[54] Vattimo's view of the relationship between God and the world appears to be even more compatible with Abe's above views specifically when Vattimo writes in an almost Zen-like fashion of the necessity to deny God (or at least what the natural religious mentality believed God to be):

> The whole relationship between God and the world must be seen from the perspective of kenosis, that is, of the dilution, weakening and denial of what the natural religious mentality believed to be God, then the Christian vision of God and humanity can face the process of demythification without fear of its essential content being disfigured or lost.[55]

It has been shown that Vattimo's kenosis contains a dynamism based on an improper *Verwindung*, which can never result in scientific or metaphysical statements. The emptying of the subject of subjective certitudes about belief in any sort of truth is similar to Abe's dynamic *śūnyatā*. In general, Zen Buddhism rejects the Hindu notion of *ātman* (inner self) as the absolute self and argues for no self (*anātman*; Japanese *muga*). This does not mean that people should have no self. Nishida's point that the self is not like a brand mark on a sheep (he refers here to William James), but "that which has its form as negating unity of the self-expressing phenomena of consciousness" makes this clear.[56] For Nishida the self is a matter of character and personality. It is better to say that there should be no "self-centeredness," which, in religion, would be the consciousness of being the "chosen people" or of having scientifically established truths, etc. This self-centeredness needs to be weakened.

Like for the above Japanese thinkers, in Vattimo's philosophy, the devoiding of the subject through *Verwindung* is a dynamic process and not a

52. Vattimo, "Age of Interpretation," 47.
53. Vattimo, "Age of Interpretation," 47; emphasis in original.
54. Vattimo, "Age of Interpretation," 47–48.
55. Vattimo, *After Christianity*, 59.
56. Nishida, *Intelligibility and the Philosophy*, 189.

definite outcome. However, it still needs to be examined whether the love and charity brought about by kenosis in Vattimo's sense are in any way similar to *śūnyatā* in the sense of nothingness. What is the element that remains once the self has gone through the process of negation with the help of kenosis and *śūnyatā*? To answer this question one needs to look at the relationship between science and religion.

4. THE EMPTYING OF GOD

Like Vattimo's, Abe's unorthodox understanding of kenosis is thinkable only in the context of non-monotheistic pluralism. Under these circumstances, discourses on the "subject" will adopt a paradoxical character for both philosophers. Abe expresses this by using the kenosis theme. When God is the son and at the same time God, we face a paradox expressed as follows: "The Son of God is not the Son of God (for he is essentially and fundamentally self-emptying): precisely because he is *not* the Son of God he is truly the Son of God."[57] Even more radically, Abe writes in *Buddhism and Interfaith Dialogue*: "Without the kenosis of God Himself, the kenosis of Christ is inconceivable," because otherwise there will be no dynamic identity of kenosis.[58] By eliminating any trace of dualism (between God and the other, the infinite and the finite, immutability and change, within and without), Abe collides with traditional Christian theology, which generally states that the Son of God became a human *without* God ceasing to be God. Abe points to Küng's statement that "we should not of course speak of a 'crucified God.' . . . Without the self-emptying of God 'the Father,' the self-emptying of the son of God is inconceivable."[59]

Vattimo is clearly on Abe's side as he suggests a concept of God that is less radical, but still very similar to Abe's "God of love" who is "not a self-affirmative God":[60]

> Kenosis, the abasement of God, is realized more and more fully and so undermines the wisdom of the world, the metaphysical dreams of natural reason which conceive God as absolute, omnipotent and transcendent, as *ipsum esse (metaphysicum) subsistens*.

---

57. Abe, "Kenotic God and Dynamic Śūnyatā," 11; emphasis in original.
58. Abe, *Buddhism and Interfaith Dialogue*, xvii.
59. Abe, *Buddhism and Interfaith Dialogue*, 14.
60. Abe, *Buddhism and Interfaith Dialogue*, 16.

> In this light, secularization—the progressive dissolution of the natural sacred—is the very essence of Christianity.[61]

Abe's kenotic God is able to overcome Christianity's monotheistic character "by sharing with Buddhism the realization of absolute nothingness."[62] In the view of Christian theologian Schubert Ogden, Abe's Buddhist adoption of kenosis is guilty of imposing Buddhism upon Christianity and of producing a concept of God that "is not only not necessarily implied by Christian faith but also necessarily precluded by it" insofar as Christian faith is faith in God's unconditional love, and this, in turn, requires both deep relatedness and duality.[63] The problem is that for Abe, the love and the fullness obtained through negation are not supposed to be "something," though most Christian commentators of Abe seem to believe that it is. Vattimo, on the other hand, comes close to Abe when he points out that if we want to understand "the gospel in today's day and age, one must first understand that language does not only denote objective realities."[64] Most theologians mentioned in the present chapter prefer to understand "fullness" in a positive sense. Heisig has referred to this danger very early: "There lurks in the background the supposition that the 'pouring out' of self only serves the higher purpose of being 'filled up' with the 'fullness' of God."[65] If this is the case, weak thought will become strong thought.

5. EMPTINESS AND FULLNESS

How precisely must "negativity" be understood in Abe's philosophy? What is the element obtained through kenosis or *śūnyatā*? While this question has worried theologians and while satisfactory answers have rarely been provided, Abe's statement on the last page of Christopher Ives's *Divine Emptiness and Historical Fullness* clarifies the situation:

> In Christian faith in Christ, the kenosis of the Son of God is not exhausted with the obedience to God the Father, but it includes the pleroma, the fullness of God. I am afraid that Pannenberg overlooks this important aspect of the notion of kenosis. And

---

61. Vattimo, *After Christianity*, 49–50.
62. Abe, "Kenotic God and Dynamic *Śūnyatā*," 17.
63. Ogden, "Faith in God," 129–30.
64. Vattimo, "Toward a Nonreligious Christianity," 38.
65. Heisig, "East-West Dialogue," 215.

this is strikingly similar to the Buddhist notion of *śūnyatā*, that is, emptiness that is identical with fullness. Mahayana Buddhism emphasizes "True emptiness is wondrous beings" and in nothingness, everything is contained.[66]

Kenosis does not lead through an act of emptying towards fullness, but it leads towards a state where emptiness and fullness cannot be distinguished; just like awakening does not lead from *saṃsāra* to *nirvāṇa* but to a state where *saṃsāra* and *nirvāṇa* are indistinct. Nishida's view of kenosis depicts the paradox contained in this constellation. It insists, like Abe's, on the fact that God's emptying itself signifies precisely "God's creating and redeeming the world out of love." It proves that the nonduality of *saṃsāra* and *nirvāṇa* cannot be framed in Western logic.[67]

The subject of emptiness and fullness has also been dealt with by Shizuteru Ueda in his essay "Leere und Fülle: Shūnyatā im Mahāyāna Buddhismus" where he insists that negation leads to a "fuller" understanding of the world, though "fuller" not in an empirical sense. Finally, the story told by Fritz Buri about how two Japanese drink tea together makes clear that emptiness should not lead to any kind of fullness:

> One says to the other: "The All is restlessly present here in a cup of tea." Whereupon the other turns over the cup so that the tea spills out and asks: "Where is the All now?" At the answer of the first, "Oh pity for a cup of such fine tea," the "two laugh at one another."[68]

Also Vattimo's nihilistic hermeneutics frees us from foundations and emancipates us without offering us something "positive" in return. What remains is the *Verwindung* of belief, which leads to a freedom not in the sense of an irrational leap of faith (which depends on an empirical understanding of "fullness"), but to dialogue, agreement, and caritas. Vattimo would probably call the empirical fullness "kitsch" in the sense of the "classically perfect identification between content and form, and the completeness and definitive quality of the work . . . (nowadays only merchandise promoted in advertising is presented in this way)."[69] We are also reminded of Roland Barthes, who saw Western metaphysics "for which every center

---

66. Abe, "God's Total Kenosis," 258.
67. Nishida, *Last Writings*, 70.
68. Buri, *Buddha-Christus*, 283.
69. Vattimo, *Beyond Interpretation*, 89.

is a place of truth" as a society striving for "the superb plenitude of reality."[70] Correspondingly, Frascati Lochhead describes a kind of religious kitsch as the "contemplation of self-fulfilling plenitude, of presence completely enfleshed, of wholeness."[71]

The above unity and feeling of oneness with God is different from the oneness of Zen-Buddhism. As mentioned, the "realism" of Buddhism is not faith lost in a foggy *nirvāṇa* but, on the contrary, the aim of Zen-Buddhism is to recognize the true character of reality. The seventeenth-century Japanese poet Basho wrote accordingly:

> You can learn about the pine tree or about the bamboo only from bamboo. When you see an object you must leave your subjective preoccupation with yourself; otherwise you impose yourself upon the object and do not learn. The object and yourself must become one, and from that feeling of oneness issues your poetry.[72]

Western objectivism and empiricism are not based on this principle of emptiness but on an objective and empirical fullness.

6. THE HUMAN AND THE DIVINE

In his rejoinder to the criticism drafted by theologians in Cobb and Ives's volume from 1990, Abe insists that we should not confuse the horizontal and the vertical dimensions of thought: "Moral difference in the sociohistorical dimension does not translate *directly* to the religious, eternal dimension." Abe quotes from Ogden's chapter in the same book and finds that for this author "the absolute moral difference does not or should not cease to make a difference but should continue to be an 'absolute difference' in the light of divine providence and divine justice."[73] Ogden had expressed his reservations towards the claim that "'dynamic *śūnyatā*' provides an adequate ground for responsible thought in history."[74] Also Ives reproaches Abe on the confusion of the categories of religion and ethics,[75] to which Abe replies that it is rather Ives who "absolutizes ethical judgment

---

70. Barthes, *Empire of Signs*, 767.
71. Frascati Lochhead, *Kenosis and Feminist Theology*, 177.
72. Yuasa, "Introduction," 18.
73. Abe, "Rejoinder" (1990), 183; emphasis in original.
74. Ogden, "Faith in God," 131.
75. Abe, "Rejoinder" (1995), 185–87.

somewhat apart from the religious dimension" and insists that a person is always living at the intersection of the vertical and horizontal dimensions.[76] Somehow, this is confusing because in the 1990 rejoinder Abe had clearly said that the horizontal and the vertical should remain separated. Those thoughts can be clarified through a comparison with Vattimo's thoughts on the same topic.

It seems that Abe and Vattimo stand on different altars but preach the same strategy. Abe regrets that the religious realm of *nirvāṇa* is interpreted by those Western theologians in sociohistorical terms while Vattimo finds that theology has brought too much science into religion. Both want to preserve the vertical dimension of religion and avoid the squaring of the circle, which attempts to see the vertical as the horizontal. The absolute must remain the absolute just because it *cannot* be expressed in terms of social ethics or science. This is the metaphysical (or anti-metaphysical) aspect of *śūnyatā*, which was very much on Nishitani's agenda. His aim was not merely to delve into the ground of human existence, but also to search "anew for the wellsprings of reality itself."[77] Therefore, a question such as "Who would raise Jesus if God was emptied?" imports historical cause and effect series into religion, which Abe, of course, has to reject.[78]

In this context, Abe's appeal that "Buddhists must develop dynamic *śūnyatā* and create a new notion of justice on the basis of wisdom and compassion, which, while clearly realizing distinctions, can actualize and maintain the balance of power" does indeed appear like a "weak thought."[79] The "confusion of the socio-historical dimension and the religious dimension and the lack of any dialectical understanding of the two dimensions" criticized by Abe is precisely the point that Vattimo also takes issue with, though he expresses it in a converse fashion.[80] Abe attacks those who import religious distinctions into the sociohistorical world while Vattimo attacks those who import sociohistorical (scientific) distinctions into religion. Again, both philosophers' aim is *not* to defend religion as an otherworldly affair, but to defend *reality*, as Abe writes: "Buddhism never asserts that distinctions are unreal or delusory in the socio-historical dimension, for if they were unreal or delusory this world would be chaotic and the

---

76. Abe, "Rejoinder" (1995), 203.
77. Nishitani, *Religion and Nothingness*, xlviii.
78. See Abe, "Beyond Buddhism," 226.
79. Abe, "Rejoinder" (1990), 180.
80. Abe, "Rejoinder" (1990), 199.

interdependency of everything would be inconceivable."[81] The appeal to *śūnyatā* or kenosis has repercussions on the balance of power in the "real" sociohistorical world. However, if kenosis and *śūnyatā* are supposed to really function, *the realms of the immanent and the transcendent must remain distinct*. In Vattimo's terms, there should never be religion in science or science in religion.

What we obtain once we apply Abe's and Vattimo's philosophies to the real world is a weakening of thought through kenosis or the awareness of *śūnyatā* in the sense of nothingness. In other words, we obtain a different relationship with reality as well as a different way of using power within this reality. This is what Vattimo means when he says that kenosis refers to secularization: only when strong structures such as the essence and the fulfilment of the Christian message are weakened will we find a truth. We need the abasement, humiliation, and weakening of God. Similarly, Abe says that "religion beyond rigid ethical judgment can provide a new basis for ethical judgment without falling into the existential dilemma of good concerning evil."[82] The call for charity and love put forward by both Abe and Vattimo can thus be defined as a call for social engagement based on a religious ground: "In order for Buddhism to be active in the contemporary world situation, it must be more theologically and practically involved in particular social-historical events from its religious grounds."[83]

CONCLUSION

We have read Vattimo through Buddhist philosophy and Abe through a postmodern philosophy of deconstruction. The comparative study has shown that the kenosis-*śūnyatā* discussion can benefit from a post-metaphysical reading based on the premises of Vattimo's weak theology. Employing a more sophisticated version of nihilism that is clearly distinct from the "modern" nihilism designed by Nietzsche and Heidegger, Abe's and Vattimo's nonreligious or secular forms of religion are relatively efficient when it comes to the deconstruction of religious fundamentalism that is more and more present in the world since the 1990s. As I mentioned, the idea of a strong and strengthening God typical for monotheistic religions clashes with the Buddhist prerogative of impermanence and non-substantiality.

81. Abe, "Rejoinder" (1990), 199.
82. Abe, "Rejoinder" (1990), 182.
83. Abe, "Rejoinder" (1990), 184.

PART II. KENOSIS IN THE KYOTO SCHOOL

Since the 1990s, religious fundamentalism has pushed forward a "religion as science" hypothesis, and both Vattimo and Abe address these problems. The idea of nothingness, which both thinkers (directly or indirectly) incorporate into their thinking, can function as a remedy against fundamentalist absolutes. Both philosophers see emptiness or nothingness not as merely nihilistic but in terms of a dynamic open-endedness. In the end, nothingness creates a "real" religious feeling. The irony and "half belief" inherent in weak thought as well as in Abe's theology circumvents metaphysical realism as well as Platonic essentialism. Irony and "half belief" are suitable measures for a situation in which "belief" or "nonbelief" are increasingly defined as an either/or. Scientism and nihilism are not the only alternatives to faith. A "half-theistic" way of thinking God based on kenosis can work in the service of plurality because it deconstructs the principle of reality based on faith and "fullness." The chapter has shown that "Eastern" and "Western" traditions can here concur.

BIBLIOGRAPHY

Abe, Masao. "Beyond Buddhism and Christianity: 'Dazzling Darkness.'" In *Divine Emptiness and Historical Fullness: A Buddhist-Jewish-Christian Conversation with Masao Abe*, edited by Christopher Ives, 224–43. Valley Forge, PA: Trinity, 1995.

———. *Buddhism and Interfaith Dialogue: Part 1 of a 2-Volume Sequel to "Zen and Western Thought."* Honolulu: University of Hawaii Press, 1995.

———. "God's Total Kenosis and Truly Redemptive Love." In *Divine Emptiness and Historical Fullness: A Buddhist-Jewish-Christian Conversation with Masao Abe*, edited by Christopher Ives, 251–59. Valley Forge, PA: Trinity, 1995.

———. "Kenotic God and Dynamic Śūnyatā." In *The Emptying God: A Buddhist-Jewish-Christian Conversation*, edited by John B. Cobb Jr. and Christopher Ives, 3–67. Maryknoll, NY: Orbis, 1990.

———. "Nishida's Philosophy of Place." *International Philosophical Quarterly* 28 (1988) 355–71.

———. "A Rejoinder." In *Divine Emptiness and Historical Fullness: A Buddhist-Jewish-Christian Conversation with Masao Abe*, edited by Christopher Ives, 175–204. Valley Forge, PA: Trinity, 1995.

———. "A Rejoinder." In *The Emptying God: A Buddhist-Jewish-Christian Conversation*, edited John B. Cobb Jr. and Christopher Ives, 157–200. Maryknoll, NY: Orbis, 1990.

———. "Will, Śūnyatā, and History." In *The Religious Philosophy of Nishitani: Encounter with Emptiness*, edited by Taitetsu Unno, 273–304. Fremont, CA: Jain, 1989.

Barthes, Roland. *Empire of Signs*. New York: Hill & Wang, 1994.

Botz-Bornstein, Thorsten. *The Philosophy of Lines: From Art Nouveau to Cyberspace*. New York: Palgrave, 2021.

Brück, Michael von. "Buddhist Shunyata and the Christian Trinity: The Emerging Holistic Paradigm." In *Buddhist Emptiness and Christian Trinity: Essays and Exploration*, edited by Roger Corless and Paul F. Knitter, 64–66. Mahwah, NJ: Paulist, 1990.

Buri, Fritz. *Der Buddha-Christus als der Herr des wahren Selbst: Die Religionsphilosophie der Kyoto-Schule und das Christentum*. Bern: Haupt, 1976.

Cabanne, E. D. "Beyond Kenosis: New Foundations for Buddhist-Christian Dialogue." *Buddhist-Christian Studies* 13 (1993) 103–17.

Caputo, John D. "Spectral Hermeneutics: On the Weakness of God and the Theology of the Event." In *After the Death of God*, by John D. Caputo and Gianni Vattimo, edited by Jeffrey W. Robbins, 47–87. Insurrections: Critical Studies in Religion, Politics, and Culture. New York: Columbia University Press, 2007.

Chappell, David W. "Introduction." In *Divine Emptiness and Historical Fullness: A Buddhist-Jewish-Christian Conversation with Masao Abe*, edited by Christopher Ives, 1–21. Valley Forge, PA: Trinity, 1995.

Coakley, Sarah. *Powers and Submissions: Spirituality, Philosophy and Gender*. Challenges in Contemporary Theology. Oxford: Blackwell, 2002.

Cobb, John B., Jr. "On the Deepening of Buddhism." In *The Emptying God: A Buddhist-Jewish-Christian Conversation*, edited by John B. Cobb Jr. and Christopher Ives, 91–101. Maryknoll, NY: 1990.

———. "Preface." In *The Emptying God: A Buddhist-Jewish-Christian Conversation*, edited by John B. Cobb Jr. and Christopher Ives, ix–xi. Maryknoll, NY: Orbis, 1990.

Cobb, John B., Jr., and Christopher Ives, eds. *The Emptying God: A Buddhist-Jewish-Christian Conversation*. Maryknoll, NY: Orbis, 1990.

Corless, Roger, and Paul F. Knitter, eds. *Buddhist Emptiness and Christian Trinity: Essays and Exploration*. Mahwah, NJ: Paulist, 1990.

Dilworth, David A. "Nishida's Critique of the Religious Consciousness." In *Last Writings Nothingness and the Religious Worldview*, by Nishida Kitarō, translated by David A. Dilworth, 1–45. Honolulu: University of Hawaii Press, 1987.

Fowl, Stephen E. *Philippians*. Two Horizons New Testament Commentary. Grand Rapids: Eerdmans, 2005.

Frascati Lochhead, Marta. *Kenosis and Feminist Theology: The Challenge of Gianni Vattimo*. Mcgill Stud Hist Religion (Dis). Albany: SUNY Press, 1998.

Heidegger, Martin. "Anaximander's Saying." In *Off the Beaten Track*, edited and translated by Julian Young and Kenneth Haynes, 242–81. Cambridge: Cambridge University Press, 2002.

———. *Being and Time*. Translated by John Macquarrie and Edward Robinson. Oxford: Blackwell, 1980.

———. *Identität und Differenz*. Vol. 11 of *Gesamtausgabe 1*. Frankfurt: Klostermann, 2006.

———. *Identity and Difference*. Translated by Joan Stambaugh. Chicago: University of Chicago Press, 1969.

———. *Nietzsche*. 2 vols. Pfullingen, Germ.: Neske, 1961.

———. *Nietzsche*. 2 vols. Translated by David Farrrell Krell. New York: Harper and Row, 1979.

———. "Overcoming Metaphysics." In *The End of Philosophy*, translated by Joan Stambaugh, 84–110. New York: Harper and Row, 1973.

———. *Sein und Zeit*. Tübingen: Niemeyer, 1986.

PART II. KENOSIS IN THE KYOTO SCHOOL

———."Der Spruch des Anaximander." In *Holzwege*, 321–73. Frankfurt: Klostermann, 1980.

———."Die Überwindung der Metaphysik" [Overcoming metaphysics]. In *Vorträge und Aufsätze*, 67–96. Pfullingen, Germ.: Neske, 1985.

Heisig, James W. "East-West Dialogue: *Śūnyatā* and Kenosis, Part 2." *Spirituality Today* 39 (1987) 211–24.

Hisamatsu, Shin'ichi. *Zen and the Fine Arts*. Tokyo: Kodansha, 1971.

Ives, Christopher, ed. *Divine Emptiness and Historical Fullness: A Buddhist-Jewish-Christian Conversation with Masao Abe*. Valley Forge, PA: Trinity, 1995.

———. "Introduction." In *The Emptying God: A Buddhist-Jewish-Christian Conversation*, edited by John B. Cobb Jr. and Christopher Ives, xii–xix. Maryknoll, NY: Orbis, 1990.

Jones, Charles B. "Emptiness, Kenosis, History, and Dialogue: The Christian Response to Masao Abe's Notion of 'Dynamic *Śūnyatā*' in the Early Years of the Abe-Cobb Buddhist-Christian Dialogue." *Buddhist-Christian Studies* 24 (2004) 117–33.

Küng, Hans. "God's Self-Renunciation and Buddhist Emptiness: A Christian Response to Masao Abe." In *Divine Emptiness and Historical Fullness: A Buddhist-Jewish-Christian Conversation with Masao Abe*, edited by Christopher Ives, 207–23. Valley Forge, PA: Trinity, 1995.

Moltmann, Jürgen. "God Is Unselfish Love." In *The Emptying God: A Buddhist-Jewish-Christian Conversation*, edited by John B. Cobb Jr. and Christopher Ives, 116–24. Maryknoll, NY: Orbis, 1990.

Nishida, Kitaro. *Intelligibility and the Philosophy of Nothingness*. Tokyo: Maruzen, 1958.

———. *Last Writings: Nothingness and the Religious Worldview*. Translated by David A. Dilworth. Honolulu: University of Hawaii Press, 1987.

Nishitani, Keiji. *Nishida Kitarō*. Berkeley: University of California Press, 1991.

———. *Religion and Nothingness*. Translated by Jan van Bragt. Nanzan Studies in Religion and Culture. Berkeley: University of California Press, 1982.

———. 宗教とは何か [*Shūkyō to wa nani ka*] [Religion and nothingness]. Tokyo: Shobunsha, 1961.

Odin, Steve. "A Critique of the '*Kenōsis/Śūnyatā*' Motif in Nishida and the Kyoto School." *Buddhist-Christian Studies* 9 (1989) 71–86.

———. *The Social Self in Zen and American Pragmatism*. Constructive Postmod Tht (Dis). Albany: SUNY Press, 1996.

Ogden, Schubert M. "Faith in God and Realization of Emptiness." In *The Emptying God: A Buddhist-Jewish-Christian Conversation*, edited by John B. Cobb Jr. and Christopher Ives, 125–34. Maryknoll, NY: Orbis, 1990.

Suzuki, Daisetz T. *Mysticism: Christian and Buddhist*. London: Psychology, 2002.

Takeuchi, Yoshinori. *The Heart of Buddhism: In Search of the Timeless Spirit of Primitive Buddhism*. New York: Crossroad, 1991.

Ueda, Shizuteru. "Leere und Fülle: Shūnyatā im Mahāyāna Buddhismus." *Eranos* 45 (1976) 135–63.

Vattimo, Gianni. *After Christianity*. New York: Columbia University Press, 1999.

———. "The Age of Interpretation." In *Richard Rorty and Gianni Vattimo: The Future of Religion*, edited by Santiago Zabala, translated by William McCuaig, 43–54. New York: Columbia University Press, 2005.

———. *Belief*. Translated by Luca D'Isanto and David Webb. Cultural Memory in the Present. Stanford, CA: Stanford University Press, 2002.

———. *Beyond Interpretation. The Meaning of Hermeneutics for Philosophy.* Oxford: Polity, 1997.

———. *Credere di credere.* Milan: Garzanti, 1996.

———. "Dialectics, Difference, Weak Thought." In *Weak Thought*, edited by Gianni Vattimo and Pier Aldo Rovatti, translated by Peter Carravetta, 39–52. Contemporary Italian Philosophy. Albany: SUNY Press, 2012.

———. "Nihilism as Emancipation." In *Cosmos and History: The Journal of Natural and Social Philosophy* 5 (2009) 19–23.

———. "A Prayer for Silence: Dialogue with Gianni Vattimo." In *After the Death of God*, by John D. Caputo and Gianni Vattimo, edited by Jeffrey W. Robbins, 89–113. Insurrections: Critical Studies in Religion, Politics, and Culture. New York: Columbia University Press, 2007. New York: Columbia University Press, 2007.

———. "Toward a Nonreligious Christianity." In *After the Death of God*, by John D. Caputo and Gianni Vattimo, edited by Jeffrey W. Robbins, 27–46. Insurrections: Critical Studies in Religion, Politics, and Culture. New York: Columbia University Press, 2007. New York: Columbia University Press, 2007.

———. *The Transparent Society.* Parallax: Re-Visions of Culture and Society. Baltimore: Johns Hopkins University Press, 1992.

———. "*Verwindung*: Nihilism and the Postmodern in Philosophy." *SubStance* 16 (1987) 7–17. https://doi.org/10.2307/3685157.

Vattimo, Gianni, and René Girard. *Christianity, Truth, and Weakening Faith: A Dialogue.* Edited by Pierpaolo Antonello. Translated by William McCuaig. New York: Columbia University Press, 2010.

Yuasa, Noboyuki. "Introduction." In *The Year of My Life: A Translation of Issa's "Oraga Haru,"* translated by Noboyuki Yuasa, 1–20. Berkeley: University of California Press, 1960.

Zabala, Santiago, ed. *Weakening Philosophy: Essays in Honour of Gianni Vattimo.* Montreal: McGill-Queen's University Press, 2006.

www.ingramcontent.com/pod-product-compliance
Lightning Source LLC
Chambersburg PA
CBHW060822190426
43197CB00038B/2182